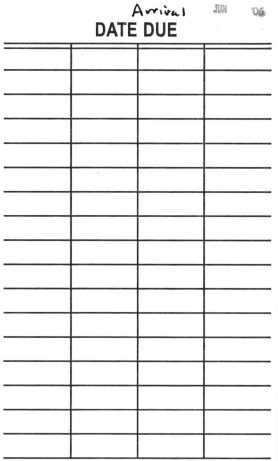

Arrival   JUN   '06
DATE DUE

Media Bias

POINT // ///// COUNTERPOINT

Affirmative Action
Amateur Athletics
American Military Policy
Animal Rights
Capital Punishment
DNA Evidence
Election Reform
Fetal Rights
Freedom of Speech
Gay Rights
Gun Control
Immigration Policy
Legalizing Marijuana
Mandatory Military Service
Media Bias
Mental Health Reform
Open Government
Physician-Assisted Suicide
Policing the Internet
Protecting Ideas
Religion in Public Schools
Rights of Students
Search and Seizure
Smoking Bans
The FCC and Regulating Indecency
The Right to Privacy
Tort Reform
Trial of Juveniles as Adults
The War on Terror
Welfare Reform

Media Bias

Paul Ruschmann, J.D.

SERIES CONSULTING EDITOR
Alan Marzilli, M.A., J.D.

CHELSEA HOUSE
PUBLISHERS
A Haights Cross Communications Company ®

Philadelphia

CHELSEA HOUSE PUBLISHERS

VP, NEW PRODUCT DEVELOPMENT   Sally Cheney
DIRECTOR OF PRODUCTION   Kim Shinners
CREATIVE MANAGER   Takeshi Takahashi
MANUFACTURING MANAGER   Diann Grasse

Staff for MEDIA BIAS

EXECUTIVE EDITOR   Lee Marcott
EDITORIAL ASSISTANT   Carla Greenberg
PHOTO EDITOR   Sarah Bloom
PRODUCTION EDITOR   Bonnie Cohen
SERIES AND COVER DESIGNER   Keith Trego
LAYOUT   21st Century Publishing and Communications, Inc.

A Haights Cross Communications ✦ Company ®

http://www.chelseahouse.com

First Printing

1 3 5 7 9 8 6 4 2

Library of Congress Cataloging-in-Publication Data

Ruschmann, Paul.
   Media bias/Paul Ruschmann.
      p. cm.—(Point counterpoint)
   Includes bibliographical references and index.
   ISBN 0-7910-8644-5 (hard cover)
   1. Journalism—Objectivity—United States. I. Title. II. Series.
PN4888.O25R87 2005
302.23'0973—dc22
                                              2005011385

CONTENTS

Foreword
Alan Marzilli, M.A., J.D.
Durham, North Carolina

The debates presented in POINT/COUNTERPOINT are among the most interesting and controversial in contemporary American society, but studying them is more than an academic activity. They affect every citizen; they are the issues that today's leaders debate and tomorrow's will decide. The reader may one day play a central role in resolving them.

Why study both sides of the debate? It's possible that the reader will not yet have formed any opinion at all on the subject of this volume—but this is unlikely. It is more likely that the reader will already hold an opinion, probably a strong one, and very probably one formed without full exposure to the arguments of the other side. It is rare to hear an argument presented in a balanced way, and it is easy to form an opinion on too little information; these books will help to fill in the informational gaps that can never be avoided. More important, though, is the practical function of the series: Skillful argumentation requires a thorough knowledge of *both* sides—though there are seldom only two, and only by knowing what an opponent is likely to assert can one form an articulate response.

Perhaps more important is that listening to the other side sometimes helps one to see an opponent's arguments in a more human way. For example, Sister Helen Prejean, one of the nation's most visible opponents of capital punishment, has been deeply affected by her interactions with the families of murder victims. Seeing the families' grief and pain, she understands much better why people support the death penalty, and she is able to carry out her advocacy with a greater sensitivity to the needs and beliefs of those who do not agree with her. Her relativism, in turn, lends credibility to her work. Dismissing the other side of the argument as totally without merit can be too easy—it is far more useful to understand the nature of the controversy and the reasons *why* the issue defies resolution.

The most controversial issues of all are often those that center on a constitutional right. The Bill of Rights—the first ten amendments to the U.S. Constitution—spells out some of the most fundamental rights that distinguish the governmental system of the United States from those that allow fewer (or other) freedoms. But the sparsely worded document is open to interpretation, and clauses of only a few words are often at the heart of national debates. The Bill of Rights was meant to protect individual liberties; but the needs of some individuals clash with those of society as a whole, and when this happens someone has to decide where to draw the line. Thus the Constitution becomes a battleground between the rights of individuals to do as they please and the responsibility of the government to protect its citizens. The First Amendment's guarantee of "freedom of speech," for example, leads to a number of difficult questions. Some forms of expression, such as burning an American flag, lead to public outrage—but nevertheless are said to be protected by the First Amendment. Other types of expression that most people find objectionable, such as sexually explicit material involving children, are not protected because they are considered harmful. The question is not only where to draw the line, but how to do this without infringing on the personal liberties on which the United States was built.

The Bill of Rights raises many other questions about individual rights and the societal "good." Is a prayer before a high school football game an "establishment of religion" prohibited by the First Amendment? Does the Second Amendment's promise of "the right to bear arms" include concealed handguns? Is stopping and frisking someone standing on a corner known to be frequented by drug dealers a form of "unreasonable search and seizure" in violation of the Fourth Amendment? Although the nine-member U.S. Supreme Court has the ultimate authority in interpreting the Constitution, its answers do not always satisfy the public. When a group of nine people—sometimes by a five-to-four vote—makes a decision that affects the lives of hundreds of millions, public outcry can be expected. And the composition of the Court does change over time, so even a landmark decision is not guaranteed to stand forever. The limits of constitutional protection are always in flux.

These issues make headlines, divide courts, and decide elections. They are the questions most worthy of national debate, and this series aims to cover them as thoroughly as possible. Each volume sets out some of the key arguments surrounding a particular issue, even some views that most people consider extreme or radical—but presents a balanced perspective on the issue. Excerpts from the relevant laws and judicial opinions and references to central concepts, source material, and advocacy groups help the reader to explore the issues even further and to read "the letter of the law" just as the legislatures and the courts have established it.

It may seem that some debates—such as those over capital punishment and abortion, debates with a strong moral component—will never be resolved. But American history offers numerous examples of controversies that once seemed insurmountable but now are effectively settled, even if only on the surface. Abolitionists met with widespread resistance to their efforts to end slavery, and the controversy over that issue threatened to cleave the nation in two; but today public debate over the merits of slavery would be unthinkable, though racial inequalities still plague the nation. Similarly unthinkable at one time was suffrage for women and minorities, but this is now a matter of course. Distributing information about contraception once was a crime. Societies change, and attitudes change, and new questions of social justice are raised constantly while the old ones fade into irrelevancy.

Whatever the root of the controversy, the books in POINT/ COUNTERPOINT seek to explain to the reader the origins of the debate, the current state of the law, and the arguments on both sides. The goal of the series is to inform the reader about the issues facing not only American politicians, but all of the nation's citizens, and to encourage the reader to become more actively involved in resolving these debates, as a voter, a concerned citizen, a journalist, an activist, or an elected official. Democracy is based on education, and every voice counts—so every opinion must be an informed one.

———————•————————•————————•———————

This volume asks whether Americans can trust newspapers, television, and other media to report the truth, or whether media outlets distort stories to achieve their own ends. Conservatives frequently charge that the media have a "liberal bias"—pointing out that reporters tend to have liberal viewpoints on welfare, abortion, and gay rights. However, most popular news outlets are owned by major corporations, and some liberals accuse the media of running stories favorable to corporate, and perhaps conservative, interests. Recently, media ownership regulations have been relaxed, further concentrating media outlets under powerful corporations. The question of whether the media is biased is important because polls indicate that Americans' beliefs are shaped by news coverage. Recently, political "blogs" have become immensely popular, but are they a means of curbing media bias or perpetuating it? This volume examines whether media bias is a widespread problem and whether corporate ownership plays a role.

Fairness, Politics, and American Media

During the 2004 presidential campaign, CBS's *60 Minutes II* news magazine program ran a story that accused President Bush of not having fulfilled his military obligations. That charge was based on Texas Air National Guard memos that were later proven to be inauthentic. The president's supporters accused CBS of trying to sabotage his reelection campaign and charged that the network ran the story because it wanted him to lose. Bush's opponents argued that CBS had gone too easy on him, not with respect just to his military record, but to his entire presidency. Although the memos were a minor issue in the campaign, the controversy over them was a perfect example of the long-running debate over media bias, or the intrusion of a journalist's views into his or her reporting.

> • **During the 2004 election campaign, which media did you rely on? Which ones did you trust?**

The Accusation: Liberal Bias

Since the 1930s, opinion polls have shown considerable public hostility toward the media, for biased coverage of politics in particular. In November 1969, Vice President Spiro Agnew put the issue on the national agenda. He charged that "a tiny, enclosed fraternity of privileged men elected by no one" had monopoly power over the news and that "the views of the majority of this fraternity do *not*—and I repeat, not—represent the views of Americans."[1] Since then, others have made similar accusations against the media. Like Agnew, they believe that the media are controlled by an elite group that has different values than most Americans and that injects its views into what is reported. Critics contend, in short, that the news is tainted by liberal bias. Others disagree. They find little solid evidence that the media distort the news and argue that biased reporting would not only endanger journalists' careers but also would quickly be exposed. They maintain not only that "liberal bias" is a myth, but also that conservatives have a strong media presence.

> • **Do you trust the media to report the news accurately? Do you think they have a hidden agenda?**

The debate over media bias is further complicated by the term *liberal*. At one point, a liberal was someone who supported limited government and free markets. The meaning of that word has changed over the years: Today, it is often used interchangeably with "left wing." Making matters worse is people's tendency to use "liberal," as well as "conservative," as "word weapons" to stereotype those who disagree with them. That said, critics of media bias generally use "liberal"

In 1969, Vice President Spiro Agnew, above, accused the media of being "a tiny, enclosed fraternity of privileged men elected by no one," who failed to reflect the views of Americans. Agnew's remarks sparked a national debate on the subject of media bias.

to mean people who are reluctant to use military force; support government regulation of the economy; favor programs to aid the poor and disadvantaged; are tolerant of abortion, homosexuality, and sex outside of marriage; and are skeptical about institutions such as religion, the military, and the traditional family.

The debate over media bias raises a number of questions: Are the news media biased? If so, which side do they favor? Does media bias affect the way Americans think and vote? There are no conclusive answers. Bias is subjective. As ABC news anchor Peter Jennings said in an interview, "I think bias is very largely in the eye of the beholder."[2] Lack of agreement as to what bias is, combined with strongly held beliefs on both sides, make it unlikely that the debate over media bias will be easily resolved.

America's Tradition of a Free Press

At the root of the debate over bias is the American political tradition, which encourages citizens to use the media as a forum for their opinions. That tradition grew out of a reaction against British colonial officials who charged their opponents with seditious libel, a crime broad enough to apply to any criticism of the government. Americans' distaste for censorship was reflected in the First Amendment to the Constitution, which states, "Congress shall make no law respecting an establishment of religion, or prohibiting the free exercise thereof; or abridging the freedom of speech, or of the press; or the right of the people peaceably to assemble, and to petition the government for a redress of grievances."[3]

The men who founded this country considered it necessary to protect the opposition press. If the government had the power to censor the opposition's press, it eventually could eliminate the opposition itself. The Founding Fathers believed that a free press was essential for the creation of a "marketplace of ideas" that would ensure a healthy, self-governing society. As Supreme Court Justice William O. Douglas stated:

> When ideas compete in the market for acceptance, full and free discussion exposes the false and they gain few adherents. Full and free discussion even of ideas we hate encourages the testing of our own prejudices and preconceptions. Full and free discussion keeps a society from becoming stagnant and unprepared for the stresses and strains that work to tear all civilizations apart.[4]

In the Founding Fathers' era, "the press" consisted of hand-printed sheets produced in small print shops. Some were newspapers; others were pamphlets or books. Printing presses were cheap enough that a person could become a publisher and editor by borrowing a few dollars for equipment and hiring an assistant or two. As a result, people with strong

The Trial of John Peter Zenger

In the eighteenth century, in both England and the American colonies, the king controlled the press through a system of licenses and restrictions. He also had the power to suppress political opponents by charging them with seditious libel—a crime that included any criticism of the king, his officials, or their policies.

A landmark seditious libel case tried in New York in 1735 helped establish America's tradition of freedom of the press. The case began when opponents of William Cosby, New York's unpopular governor, founded an independent newspaper called the *New York Weekly Journal*. The *Journal* was printed by John Peter Zenger, a German immigrant who owned a printing press.

Angered by critical stories in the *Journal*, Governor Cosby took steps to shut it down. He ordered his attorney general to issue a warrant for Zenger's arrest on seditious libel charges. Cosby also did everything he could to guarantee that Zenger would be convicted, including hand-picking the judge, barring Zenger's chosen lawyers from defending him, and even trying to stack the jury with his own supporters.

Making matters worse for Zenger was the difficulty of proving one's innocence of seditious libel. In those days, criticism of the government was against the law because it stirred up disagreements and could lead to violence. Truth was not a defense for a seditious libel charge; in fact, true statements were considered even more libelous than false ones.

The difficult task of defending Zenger fell on his new lawyer, a Philadelphian named Alexander Hamilton. Having no other alternative, Hamilton based opinions had the means of putting their thoughts into the hands of their fellow citizens.

Those who founded this country intended for political debate to be robust. Vigorous, even vicious, political campaigns were the norm in early America. As S.C. Gwynne, a former *Time* magazine reporter, observed, "In the decades after the

his defense on the controversial strategy of jury nullification—persuading the jury to find Zenger innocent not because the government failed to prove its case but because it disagreed with the law itself. Hamilton told the jury that Zenger had printed the truth and that the case was not just about him but about the cause of liberty itself. He urged the jurors to follow their consciences: "A proper confidence in a court is commendable; but as the verdict (whatever it is) will be yours, you ought to refer no part of your duty to the discretion of other persons. If you should be of the opinion that there is no falsehood in Mr. Zenger's papers, you will, nay (pardon me for the expression) you ought to say so."[*] The law was not on Zenger's side, but the jury was. It reportedly took only "a small time" to agree on a not-guilty verdict.

The Zenger case did not change the law of seditious libel, but it did send the message that colonists were against prosecuting people for it. Those sentiments motivated Congress to add the First Amendment, and its guarantee of freedom of the press, to the Constitution. Even after the Constitution was ratified, however, there were sporadic attempts by the government to punish its critics—for example, in the final years of the eighteenth century, during the Civil War, and during World War I and the years immediately after it. Nevertheless, during the middle and late twentieth century, the Supreme Court made it increasingly clear that the law could not be used to punish someone merely for criticizing the government.

[*] Alan Dershowitz, *America on Trial: Inside the Legal Battles That Transformed Our Nation.* New York: Warner Books, 2004, p. 47.

American Revolution, almost all newspapers were run by political parties. They were deeply biased and happy to fabricate lies about the opposition."[5]

The News Media Become an Industry

The economy of the nineteenth century transformed the press into something that the Founding Fathers could not have imagined: a lucrative business controlled by a wealthy and powerful elite. Several factors brought this about. Technological advances allowed the mass production of newspapers, a growing economy made advertising a new source of revenue, and more and more Americans were able to read. Newspapers became viable businesses after publishers discovered that articles about sex and crime appealed to large numbers of readers who, in turn, attracted advertisers—a formula that still works. As publishers competed aggressively for readers, the newspaper industry became concentrated: The number of papers declined, but their circulation grew.

By the late nineteenth century, few Americans could afford to become publishers. The cost of starting a competitive paper rose to the point that only wealthy individuals and large corporations could enter the business. Joseph Pulitzer, William Randolph Hearst, and other newspaper barons operated with little government regulation. "In those times, sprawling, self-interested corporations filled the void. And they weren't just depicted in the media—they were the media."[6] Corporate ownership of the media became a concern and remains one today.

Professional Standards Come to Journalism

At the turn of the twentieth century, many publishers relied on lurid stories to sell newspapers. That practice, called "yellow journalism," continues today in some media such as supermarket tabloid newspapers and television programs like *The Jerry Springer Show*. Yellow journalism came under fire from both conservatives, who objected to its coarseness, and progressives, who believed that mainstream newspapers sided with big business. A class of educated journalists called "muckrakers" offered an alternative: fact-based stories that exposed official corruption, corporate wrongdoing, and urban poverty. They were the forerunners of modern-day investigative journalists.

> • **Have the networks turned news into "infotainment"? Is there enough of an audience to support serious newscasts?**

At the same time, the economics of newspaper publishing were changing:

> Partisan journalism, the bread and butter of Jefferson, Jackson, and Lincoln, could only be defended in an environment where there were competitive markets, and a wide range of opinion. In the highly concentrated newspaper markets that emerged by the twentieth century, partisan journalism appeared more like uncontested propaganda than anything else.[7]

When publishers realized that they could not risk offending readers with opinionated writing, they adopted new standards to free editors and reporters from their control:

> Professional journalism was born from the revolutionary idea that the link between owner and editor could be broken. The news would be determined by trained professionals and the politics of owners and advertisers would be apparent only on the editorial page. Journalists would be given considerable autonomy to control the news using their professional judgment. Among other things, they would be trained to establish their political neutrality.[8]

In the early twentieth century, universities established journalism schools. Joseph Pulitzer donated part of his fortune to Columbia University to establish a school that would build an *esprit de corps* (common spirit) among journalists, like that of military academy graduates.

The Rise of the Broadcast Media

By the 1930s, radio had surpassed newspapers as Americans' mass medium of choice. The "marketplace of ideas" model proved difficult to apply to radio, however. Anyone, in theory, could start a newspaper, but not everyone could own a radio station because the portion of the electromagnetic spectrum used for radio signals was limited. Congress addressed the problem of "spectrum scarcity"—there were more would-be broadcasters than broadcast frequencies—by issuing broadcasters licenses that gave them the exclusive right to use a radio frequency in a given geographic area. In return, broadcasters were expected to use the airwaves to serve the public interest. The same model was later used for television broadcasters. By the 1960s, television had become the dominant medium. Nightly news broadcasts brought stories such as civil rights marches in the South and the fighting in Vietnam into Americans' living rooms. Many were disturbed by the images they saw.

Congress created a government agency, the Federal Communications Commission (FCC), to regulate broadcasters. To promote the public interest, the FCC adopted rules that banned obscenity and indecency, limited the number of stations a company could own, and required broadcasters to be impartial. Beginning in the 1980s, however, a philosophy of deregulation took hold. Policymakers concluded that a free market would serve the public interest better than government-imposed rules would. During the past two decades, both the FCC and Congress have loosened restrictions on owning stations.

Both conservative and liberal activists have responded by organizing campaigns against further efforts to deregulate.

"All the News That's Fit to Print"

Although today's media are vastly different from those of early America, the First Amendment still protects them. In fact, today's media enjoy even greater constitutional protection. There are relatively few legal restrictions on what a person may publish or broadcast. Forbidden categories include obscenity, false advertising, treasonous statements, words that directly incite violence, and libel. Unlike the seditious libel of colonial days, modern-day libel is a civil matter—that is, one between private parties. A person who believes that his or her reputation was harmed by a false statement can sue the person who made it. If he or she wins, the court will award a sum of money meant to make good the damage done.

The libel suits of the twentieth century, like the seditious libel prosecutions of colonial times, tended to discourage free speech. Faced with the risk of being sued, many broadcasters and publishers toned down their coverage or avoided certain stories altogether. The resulting self-censorship "chilled" speech about controversial issues and deprived the public of the robust debate the Founding Fathers intended. In *New York Times Co.* v. *Sullivan*, 376 U.S. 254 (1964), the Supreme Court addressed this problem by making it harder for public officials to win libel suits. Later, the Court gave similar protection to stories about "public figures" such as celebrities and to expressions of opinion such as political cartoons.

> • **Do the media play down stories that might embarrass their advertisers? Stories critical of government leaders?**

Other than filing a libel suit, someone who has been attacked in the media has few means of defending himself or herself. For many years, the FCC required broadcasters to make

(continued on page 22)

FROM THE BENCH

Silencing the Press: *New York Times* v. *Sullivan*

By 1960, prosecutions for seditious libel had long become a thing of the past. Public officials in some parts of the country, however, were still using the courts to silence the press. One such place was Montgomery, Alabama, where Dr. Martin Luther King, Jr., and other figures in the civil rights movement led marches and sit-ins. The national news media covered the protests, and some community leaders resented the bad publicity that they received.

On March 29, 1960, the *New York Times* ran a full-page ad that appealed to readers to support the protesters. It alleged that Dr. King and others were "being met by an unprecedented wave of terror by those who would deny and negate [the Bill of Rights]" and cited specific abuses by the police. The ad contained a number of factual errors, however. Those errors gave L.B. Sullivan, a Montgomery city commissioner who supervised the police department, a chance to retaliate against the *Times*.

Commissioner Sullivan sued the *Times,* alleging that the advertisement had libeled him. In order to win his lawsuit, Sullivan had to prove that the ad contained false statements, was "of and concerning" him, and damaged his reputation. A Circuit Court jury concluded that he had proved all three points and awarded him $500,000, the largest award in a libel case in state history. Alabama's highest court later upheld the judgment.

At the time, a newspaper that lost a libel case usually paid the judgment rather than risk losing even more money on an unsuccessful appeal. The *Times* decided not to pay. Instead, it asked the U.S. Supreme Court to review the case, in part because the newspaper feared a flood of similar suits. Another reason was that its lawyer believed that the Court was in the process of expanding First Amendment protection. The lawyer's prediction proved correct: The Supreme Court ruled unanimously that the Alabama courts had violated the *Times*'s First Amendment rights.

Justice William Brennan wrote the Court's opinion. He cited the long-standing principle that debate on public issues should be "uninhibited, robust, and wide open" and that laws that limited such debate raised First Amendment issues. He drew a parallel between Commissioner Sullivan's libel suit and the Sedition Act of 1798, a law intended to silence critics of John Adams's administration. The Court never ruled on the Sedition Act's constitutionality, but Justice Brennan found that the act had been overruled "in the court of history."

Those who were convicted were pardoned, and Congress passed legislation that repaid their fines.

Commissioner Sullivan's lawsuit was not a criminal prosecution, but Justice Brennan found that it had the potential to suppress speech. He pointed out that the damage award to Sullivan was 1,000 times larger than the maximum fine for criminal libel in Alabama and that the *Times* could be sued multiple times for the same publication. (In fact, the *Times* told the Court that it was facing 11 libel suits demanding a total of 5.6 million dollars in damages.)

Although Alabama law recognized truth as a defense in a libel case, Justice Brennan found that the defense was insufficient to protect the *Times*'s right to speak, in part because a person accused of libel had the burden of proving that he had told the truth. To make the right of free speech meaningful, Justice Brennan laid down a more restrictive standard for libel cases brought by a public official: An official may not recover "unless he proves that the statement was made with 'actual malice'—that is, with knowledge that it was false or with reckless disregard of whether it was false or not."

Finally, Justice Brennan concluded that, in any event, there was not enough evidence to support a judgment in favor of Commissioner Sullivan. He found that the *Times* was, at worst, negligent in not fact-checking the advertisement and that its staff neither knew of nor recklessly disregarded the false statements that it contained. In addition, Brennan found that the ad was not "of and concerning" Sullivan because it did not refer to him by either name or official position.

Justices Hugo Black, William O. Douglas, and Arthur Goldberg concurred. They agreed that Commissioner Sullivan should not have won the lawsuit but argued that the majority had not gone far enough in protecting free speech. They maintained that a citizen had an "unconditional privilege," or unlimited right, to criticize a public official's performance of his or her duties. In their view, an "actual malice" standard did not provide enough protection because it was uncertain and thus allowed a hostile jury to examine a speaker's motives after the fact. Justice Goldberg pointed out that, although an unconditional privilege might lead some speakers to make maliciously false statements, public officials had access to the media and thus were capable of defending themselves.

(continued from page 19)

airtime available to those individuals they attacked. That requirement was scrapped in 1987 as part of the trend toward deregulation. Newspapers have no legal obligation to allow targets of attacks to reply. Furthermore, there is no "right to be covered" either on the air on in newspapers. A person who is ignored by the media or portrayed in a true but unfavorable light has no legal recourse. In addition, there are few checks on the media. Publishers and editors are not public servants who can be voted out of office, and individual journalists are not members of a regulated profession as doctors and lawyers are. As Doris Graber, a professor of political science at the University of Illinois at Chicago, observed, "Citizens can be protected from false advertising of consumer goods through truth in advertising laws, but there is no way in which they can be protected from false political claims or improper news selection by media personnel without impairing crucial rights to free speech and a free press."[9]

> • **Should editors be required to attend journalism school? Should reporters have to take courses in ethics?**

Summary

Freedom of the press, guaranteed by the First Amendment, is a basic principle of American democracy. The Founding Fathers believed in a "marketplace of ideas" in which people with strong opinions could publish and distribute them in the hope of influencing their neighbors. The media have changed greatly over the years. Today, most newspapers and broadcast stations are in the hands of a small number of corporate owners, and media corporations deliver not only news but entertainment and advertising as well. The First Amendment gives the media broad leeway to report and comment on the news. That, combined with a "hands-off" approach by the government, leaves most targets of media bias with only one way to fight back—by appealing to public opinion.

Journalists Are Out of Touch With America

O bjectivity is the official policy of American journalism, but some allege that those who work for the media are biased and that their biases find their way into the news. One vocal critic is Bernard Goldberg, the former CBS News journalist who wrote the book *Bias*. Goldberg believes that bias occurs because those in the media have more liberal views than most Americans. He adds that they live apart from the rest of the country and that isolation blinds them to their own bias. In a column in the *Wall Street Journal*, Goldberg observed:

> The media elites can float through their personal lives and rarely run into someone with an opposing view. This is very unhealthy and sometimes downright ridiculous, as when Pauline Kael, for years the brilliant film critic at the *New*

Yorker, was completely baffled about how Richard Nixon could have beaten George McGovern in 1972: "Nobody I knew voted for Nixon." Never mind that Nixon carried 49 states. She wasn't kidding.[10]

> • **Do journalists see the world differently than your family and friends do? Do journalists understand your problems?**

A small group of people controls the media.

The term *media* refers to outlets that range from national television networks to weekly papers that serve small towns. The debate over liberal bias, however, focuses on a small group of influential media. Eric Alterman, a liberal media critic, explained:

> The relevant media are the elite national media, located largely in the networks, the nation's top five national newspapers, the newsweeklies, the opinion magazines, the executives who run these companies along with the sources, both on- and off-air, who supply them with information and opinions. With a few important exceptions, these media's inhabitants can largely be found living and working in New York or Washington, with an entertainment subsidiary in Los Angeles.[11]

Because these leading outlets are so influential, those who control them are "gatekeepers" who can shape political debate. Vice President Agnew warned his audience about the extent of media executives' power: "These men can create national issues overnight. They can make or break by their coverage and commentary a moratorium on the war. They can elevate men from obscurity to national prominence within a week. They can reward some politicians with national exposure and ignore others."[12] Years later, many believe that Agnew's words are still true.

Many contend that bias on the part of the leading outlets is magnified because editors and publishers across the country rely on elite sources to decide which stories are newsworthy. Brent Baker, an official of the conservative Media Research Center, explained:

> Consider the case of the *Dallas Morning News*. Because of the positions on its editorial page, the *News* is considered "conservative"—yet much of its national news comes straight from the New York Times News Service or the Los Angeles Times-Washington Post News Service, both of which distribute stories from those papers to newsrooms across the country.[13]

Some believe that the rise of "celebrity journalists" has added to the pack-mentality phenomenon. Professor Doris Graber observed, "If anchors Peter Jennings, Tom Brokaw, or Dan Rather declare that health care legislation will lower the quality of medical care or that an American military presence along the coast of China will risk war, popular support for these policies may plunge."[14]

Journalists are isolated from most Americans.

Critics accuse the media elite of holding different views than most Americans on social and cultural issues. According to Bernard Goldberg, "That's one of the biggest problems in big-time journalism: its elites are hopelessly out of touch with everyday Americans. Their friends are liberals, just as they are. And they share the same values. Almost all of them think the same way on the big social issues of our time: abortion, gun control, feminism, gay rights, the environment, school prayer."[15]

Some believe that the problem dates back to the 1960s, when a "New Class" arose in America. It included members of

Former NBC anchor Tom Brokaw (left) and former CBS anchor Dan Rather (center) listen as ABC anchor Peter Jennings speaks at a panel called "From Where We Sit." Critics, who have described these three as "celebrity journalists," charge that their delivery of the news can greatly affect public opinion.

well-educated elites in the law, universities, government bureaucracies, and the media. Critics accused the New Class of being disconnected from the rest of the country and lacking respect for institutions such as churches and the military. There is evidence that members of the media elite behave like members of the New Class. In 2000, Peter Brown, the *Orlando Sentinel*'s features editor, found that journalists were less likely to get married and have children, do volunteer work, and own homes than Americans in general. He also found that journalists who worked for major media outlets tended to live in upscale neighborhoods and even gated communities.

The sharpest cultural division between journalists and the rest of America involves religion. Journalists not only are less likely to go to church, but they also tend not to associate with those who do. Fred Barnes, the editor of the conservative *Weekly Standard,* described a meeting between a Republican official and the Washington staff of a national newspaper. All of the 20 or so journalists said that they knew a gay person, but only a handful said that they knew a born-again Christian. Barnes remarked, "What makes this impromptu poll so revealing is that more than 40 percent of Americans consider themselves born-again or evangelical Christians. Gays are less than five percent of the population. Yet experienced journalists well acquainted with the gay community are scarcely familiar with conservative Christians." [16]

Journalists today often are better educated than the average person. Before World War II, newspaper work was a way for working-class people to advance themselves. A college education was seldom required and was even a disadvantage in some newsrooms. In addition, journalists tend to be wealthier than most Americans. In 2002, a journalist's median salary at one of the nation's 40 largest circulation newspapers was nearly twice the median income of the average worker. John Leo, a columnist for *U.S. News & World Report,* remarked, "It used to be that anybody could be a reporter by walking in the door. It's a little harder to do that now, and you don't get the working-class Irish poor. . . . What you get is people from Ivy League colleges with upper-class credentials, what you get is people who more and more tend to be and act alike." [17]

Critics like Brent Baker add that liberal bias tends to perpetuate itself. He observed:

> The media know the liberal perspective. They have heard the
> liberal argument throughout college and journalism school.
> No doubt they continue to hear the "politically correct" side
> from their friends and colleagues in the newsrooms. On

the other hand, they are often ignorant of the conservative perspective on issues and unaware of the experts available to provide it.[18]

Journalists hold liberal views.

Conservative commentator James Glassman asserted that "the people who report the stories are liberal Democrats. This is the shameful open secret of American journalism. That the press itself . . . chooses to gloss over it is conclusive evidence of how pernicious the bias is."[19] Studies show that a substantial majority of journalists are Democrats. In 1937, author Leo Rosten surveyed reporters based in Washington, D.C.. He found that they had voted to reelect President Franklin D. Roosevelt by a wider margin than Americans as a whole. This pattern held up in the elections that followed. In 1981, S. Robert Lichter, then a professor at George Washington University, surveyed journalists at the most influential media outlets. He found that 81 percent had voted Democratic in every presidential election between 1964 and 1976. The 1972 election provided a striking contrast: 81 percent of journalists voted for George McGovern, even though Americans reelected President Nixon with 62 percent of the vote. The Freedom Forum reported that, in 1992, 89 percent of Washington bureau chiefs and congressional correspondents said that they voted for Bill Clinton, compared to only 7 percent for President George H.W. Bush.

Surveys show that, on social issues, journalists are more liberal than Americans in general. Ninety percent of those who responded to Lichter's 1981 survey favored abortion rights, and 80 percent supported "strong affirmative action" for African Americans. In 1985, the *Los Angeles Times* found that 81 percent of journalists backed affirmative action and 78 percent wanted stricter gun control. Ten years later, Stanley Rothman and Amy Black found that 73 percent of reporters and editors believed that homosexuality was as acceptable a lifestyle as heterosexuality and 75 percent thought that the government should take steps to reduce the income gap. In contrast, the number of Americans who describe themselves as "pro-life" is about the same as those who call themselves "pro-choice," most are against racial preferences and a ban on handguns, and a majority believes that President George W. Bush's tax cuts, which have mainly benefited the wealthy, should be made permanent.

Journalists describe themselves as liberal. A 1996 survey conducted by the American Society of Newspaper Editors

Measuring Liberal Bias:
Edith Efron's *The News Twisters*

As early as 1960, Republicans complained that the national television networks gave their presidential candidate less favorable coverage than his Democratic opponent received. Some even complained to the FCC about slanted coverage. At the time, the FCC enforced the Fairness Doctrine, a rule that required broadcasters to air contrasting points of view on controversial issues. That rule applied to expressions of opinion, however, not to newscasts.

Edith Efron, a staffer at *TV Guide,* believed that the networks' election coverage violated at least the spirit of the Fairness Doctrine. To prove how "severely biased" that coverage was, Efron recorded the networks' evening newscasts over the last seven weeks of the 1968 presidential campaign and counted the number of words spoken in favor of and against the major candidates. She also counted the words spoken for and against the "liberal" position on ten major issues. The technique she used is called "content analysis," a quantitative method for analyzing the communications of people and organizations. It is often used by those who seek to show biased media coverage.

Her book, *The News Twisters,* was published in 1971. It reported her findings, along with her attempt at "a coherent theory of bias." Although both Efron and her publisher were virtually unknown, they became famous in conservative circles. *The News Twisters* also proved influential: It encouraged others to follow Efron's lead and perform their own content analyses to prove that liberal bias existed.

Efron contended that there was no clear division between editorials and straight news reporting. In fact, she maintained that there was more editorializing,

(ASNE) found that 61 percent identified themselves as having liberal or Democratic leanings compared to only 15 percent with conservative or Republican leanings. In 2004, the Pew Research Center for the People and the Press found that journalists and media executives identified themselves as "liberal" (34 percent) about five times more often than as "conservative" (7 percent). About half called themselves "moderate," but conservatives contend that many in that group hold liberal views as well. In contrast, a Gallup poll taken at about the same time found that

and stronger forms of it, in the "analysis" segments of newscasts. Efron also pointed out that a news story could be factually accurate and still convey a political point of view, especially through spokespersons quoted in newscasts. She asserted that the selection of spokespersons reflected the biases of the network's editorial personnel.

Efron's main finding was that, in covering the election, the networks spoke 1,620 words in favor of Nixon and 17,027 words against him compared to 8,458 words in favor of his Democratic opponent, Hubert Humphrey, and 8,307 words against him. She argued that Nixon won the 1968 election despite the fact that the networks had "broadcast the quantitative equivalent of a *New York Times* lead editorial against him every day." Efron also found that the networks took the liberal side of the issues; for example, they spoke 700 words in favor of the administration's Vietnam policy and 3,044 words against it and 2,088 words in favor of "the Left" and 1,065 words against it.

Efron maintained that a "ruling intellectual class," which held liberal and Democratic views, dominated the broadcasting industry. To combat their bias, she called on the networks to air commentary by a "spectrum" of spokespersons who represented views from the far left to the far right and to make greater efforts to recruit conservative journalists. Efron also favored doing away with federal regulation of the broadcast industry and instead letting the marketplace decide whose views would be heard. The FCC took a major step toward deregulation in 1987 when it abolished the Fairness Doctrine.

40 percent of Americans called themselves "conservative," 40 percent "moderate," and 20 percent "liberal."

> • **Is it possible for journalists to keep their personal views out of their reporting?**

Some journalists confuse activism with reporting.

Conservatives insist that some journalists misuse their position to advance liberal views. Brent Baker argued, "Being a journalist is not like being a surveillance camera at an ATM, faithfully recording every scene for future playback. Journalists make subjective decisions every minute of their professional lives. They choose what to cover and what not to cover, which sources are credible and which are not, which quotes to use in a story and which to toss out."[20]

Some believe that an entire generation of journalists was inspired by Bob Woodward and Carl Bernstein, two investigative reporters from the *Washington Post*. They reported on the 1972 break-in at Democratic Party headquarters in the Watergate building and the Nixon administration officials' involvement in the incident and their attempt to cover it up. Critics argue that such reporting, by its very nature, leads to bias. According to Professor Graber, the investigative reporter's aims are to produce exciting stories that appeal to an audience, to gain status within the profession, and to trigger political action.

> • **Do investigative reporters do more harm than good or vice versa?**

Many people enter journalism because of a desire to improve society. Bernard Goldberg remarked, "More than ever, journalists on the Left define themselves by their compassion. They might as well wear big red buttons on their lapels that say, 'We Care.'"[21] Some journalists admit their motivation. In a televised roundtable discussion, long-time White House correspondent

Helen Thomas said, "A liberal bias? I don't know what a liberal bias is. Do you mean we care about the poor, the sick, and the maimed? Do we care whether people are being shot every day on the streets of America? If that's liberal, so be it."[22]

Critics add that mixing activism and journalism can have serious consequences. Conservative columnist Kay Daly cited

Rather Biased? CBS's "Memogate Scandal"

To the surprise of many Americans, the Vietnam War resurfaced as an issue in the 2004 presidential campaign. During the primaries and at his party's national convention, Democratic candidate John Kerry reminded voters of his tour of duty as a navy officer in Vietnam. Opponents assailed Kerry's military record. A group that called itself the Swift Boat Veterans for Truth ran television ads that accused Kerry of lying about his heroism in Vietnam and hurting the war effort by taking part in antiwar protests after leaving the navy.

At the same time, President Bush's opponents charged that his military record was flawed. Among other things, they accused his family of using its influence to get him into the Texas Air National Guard and contended that Bush had not fulfilled his National Guard duties. On September 8, 2004, CBS's *60 Minutes II* news magazine aired a story entitled "New Questions on Bush Guard Duty." Part of it was based on newly discovered memos allegedly written by Lieutenant Colonel Jerry Killian, Bush's commanding officer. The memos indicated that Bush had been suspended from flight status for missing a required physical exam and that Killian had been pressured by his higher-ups to "sugarcoat" Bush's record.

CBS did not know at the time that the memos were not authentic. The network hired experts to examine them, but the experts' areas of specialty did not extend to typesetting technology and computer fonts. Within hours of the report, conservative bloggers argued that the memos had been generated by word-processing technology that did not exist when Bush was in the National Guard. (A "blogger" is a person who maintains an online "Weblog" or "blog," a site filled with links to news stories and the blogger's commentary about them.)

Even as evidence that the memos were not authentic mounted, CBS refused to back down. Dan Rather blamed "partisan political operatives" for stories that questioned the memos. In addition, his fellow anchors, NBC's Tom Brokaw and ABC's Peter Jennings, accused critics of conducting a political vendetta against Rather and CBS. Some of those critics saw their reaction as proof not only that Brokaw and Jennings were biased but also that they were so blinded by their liberal views that they could not recognize their bias.

Adding to the controversy was the reputation of Rather himself. For years, many conservatives viewed him as the personification of liberal bias. Their hostility toward Rather dates back at least to a 1974 news conference at which he asked President Nixon a pointed question about his lack of cooperation with members of Congress who were deciding whether to impeach him. Rather had also drawn fire for an on-air confrontation with then–Vice President George H.W. Bush and for appearing at a Democratic Party function in Texas.

Media critics accused CBS of poor journalism. They charged the network with running the Bush story despite warnings that the National Guard memos might not be genuine and with taking too long to repudiate the memos after evidence of forgery appeared. Some even charged CBS with running the story in an effort to influence the election. They pointed out that the man who furnished the documents, a retired colonel named Bill Burkett, was active in Democratic politics and a known enemy of Bush; that the story's producer, Mary Mapes, had spent five years investigating Bush's National Guard service and was looking for evidence of unsatisfactory performance; and that Mapes had allegedly put Burkett in touch with a high-ranking official of the Kerry campaign.

On September 20, 2004, CBS admitted that Burkett had lied about the authenticity of the documents. That evening, Rather told his audience, "Tonight, after further investigation, we can no longer vouch for their authenticity. . . . I want to say personally and directly—I'm sorry." Two days later, CBS hired a former U.S. attorney general and a retired president of the Associated Press to investigate its handling of the Bush story.

In January 2005, the investigators released their report. They concluded that the *60 Minutes II* story was neither fair nor accurate, but they stopped short of concluding that the memos were false and they found no evidence that the story was motivated by political bias. CBS responded by firing Mapes and asking three other senior news executives to resign. The network took no action against Rather, who had already announced that he would leave the *CBS Evening News* in March 2005. Many believe that "Memogate" was the reason why he stepped down.

one example. In October 2003, the *Orlando Sentinel* ran a series of articles about the prescription painkiller OxyContin. They were written by Doris Bloodsworth, a self-described "mom with a word processor" who "always wanted to be a reporter." Bloodsworth wrote that OxyContin was responsible for 573 deaths statewide in Florida. The primary ingredient in OxyContin caused only one-fourth of those deaths, however; the rest resulted from a combination of drugs. The *Sentinel* eventually acknowledged that Bloodsworth's articles grossly overstated OxyContin deaths and were "far off the mark." In the meantime, federal and state officials proposed restrictions on the drug that could have left some patients with no effective way to relieve their chronic pain. Daly also pointed out that the maker of OxyContin had the means to fight biased coverage of its product, but many other victims do not.

Summary

Critics of liberal bias in the media point to two major reasons it exists. First, the industry is dominated by an elite group of individuals. They control the most influential media outlets, and smaller outlets follow their lead. Second, journalists have become isolated from the rest of America. They tend to be wealthier and better educated than average and live apart from and have little in common with other Americans. For years, studies have shown that journalists tend to support Democratic candidates and have liberal political views, especially on social issues. In addition, some journalists are activists who view their job as changing society rather than reporting the news.

Journalists' Views Do Not Affect Their Reporting

Assuming that reporters have liberal views, is that bias reflected in their reporting? Even if it is, does it have an effect on the political views of Americans in general? Mike Wallace, a veteran CBS journalist, believes that the effect is minimal:

> When people suggest there is a bias in the media and we have all this power and then of course the bias is always supposed to be liberal and not conservative, well then, under those circumstances how many Democratic presidents and how many Republican presidents have there been beginning with Richard Nixon.[23]

Defenders of the media accuse critics of having created the untrue and unfair impression that journalists systematically slant the news to the left.

Critics exaggerate journalists' liberal views.

Defenders of the media accuse critics of finding liberal bias where it does not exist—because it is easier to accuse someone of bias than to prove it. Bias is not only hard to define, but it also exists on the part of the audience as well as the speaker. A person who says, "he is biased" often really means "he disagrees with me." Furthermore, bias is not a trait limited to liberals. As Dick Meyer, the editorial director of CBSNews.com, explained, "Most people who are interested in news and ideas, at some point realize that everyone—even themselves—is biased. To be a human who makes judgments and uses words is to be a biased person."[24] In any event, charges of bias are as old as politics itself. They have been made by, and directed at, people everywhere on the political spectrum.

- **Is bias "in the eye of the beholder"? Can it be measured?**

Critics have been accused of focusing on a few emotional issues, such as gay rights and affirmative action, to create the impression that journalists hold left-of-center views on *every* issue. That is not necessarily true. Journalists, who earn more money than the average American, tend to hold more conservative views on economic issues. For example, most support globalization—the lowering of economic barriers between countries. Globalization has been blamed for the movement of jobs overseas and, for that reason, has been opposed by labor unions and some liberal lawmakers. For example, media coverage was overwhelmingly in favor of the North American Free Trade Agreement (NAFTA), which made it easier for Mexican and Canadian products to enter this country. Congress ratified NAFTA in 1993, and some beleive that favorable news coverage was one reason why.

Critics also wrongly assume that journalists' personal views find their way into their reporting. Everette Dennis, the former dean of Willamette University's school of journalism, maintained:

> The U.S. press is not liberal, except in the personal political views of a majority of reporters, and these characteristics are no more likely to be injected into a story than are journalists' age, educational background, religion or taste in music. But some critics fill in those blanks, manufacture connections that don't exist, and then paint their critique across the facade of an entire industry.[25]

Although journalists have been branded as "liberal," their reporting has not always been sympathetic toward left-of-center figures. Many believe that White House correspondents were very aggressive in covering the various scandals that involved President Clinton, especially his affair with White House intern Monica Lewinsky. In fact, President Clinton's harshest critics included correspondents for *Newsweek* and the *Washington Post*, two publications often described as liberal.

Finally, even if journalists do have a liberal bias, critics have exaggerated their power to influence political debate. Four Republican presidents have been elected since Vice President Agnew spoke out against the liberal media; in the 1930s and 1940s, Democrats held the White House for 20 consecutive years even though most newspapers had endorsed their Republican opponents. Professor Doris Graber adds that social changes such as the civil-rights struggle and the sexual revolution were well underway before they received serious attention in the media and that many prominent Americans came out against the Vietnam War before commentators started to criticize it.

Ethical standards discourage biased reporting.

First and foremost, a journalist is a professional. Biased

reporting violates the profession's standards. Article IV of the ASNE's Statement of Principles advises, "Good faith with the reader is the foundation of good journalism. Every effort must be made to assure that the news content is accurate, free from bias and in context, and that all sides are presented fairly." [26] In addition, good journalists are trained, both in school and on the job, to keep bias out of their reporting. Ben Bagdikian, author of *The Media Monopoly*, remarked, "Today, journalists are not only better educated, but they are more concerned with individual professional ethics than would have seemed possible 50 years ago. The conventions against lying, fictionalizing, and factual inaccuracy are strong and widespread. Collection of accurate facts is a high priority in American reporting." [27]

• Compared to other professionals, how ethical are journalists?

Other checks also minimize bias. Journalists police one another. Many outlets have media critics on their staff; the *Washington Post*'s critic, Howard Kurtz, is so influential that he has been called "the top cop on the beat." For years, journalism schools have exposed deficient and irresponsible practices; today, some schools have a presence on the Internet. FactCheck.org, sponsored by the University of Pennsylvania's Annenberg Public Policy Center, reported on untruths and distortions during the 2004 presidential campaign. Independent organizations also monitor the media for biased coverage. The Media Research Center (www.mrc.org) catalogs and reports on liberal bias, and Media Matters for America (www.mediamatters.org) does the same with respect to conservative bias. The Internet is also home to thousands of Weblogs, or "blogs," that comment on the news and criticize inaccurate reporting. Bloggers occasionally break stories not covered by the mainstream media. For example, at a birthday party for a retired lawmaker, Mississippi Senator Trent Lott

(continued on page 42)

American Society of Newspaper Editors Statement of Principles

In 1922, the American Society of Newspaper Editors adopted its first "Canons of Journalism." They were revised and renamed "Statement of Principles" in 1975 and were most recently updated in August 2002.*

> **PREAMBLE.** The First Amendment, protecting freedom of expression from abridgment by any law, guarantees to the people through their press a constitutional right, and thereby places on newspaper people a particular responsibility. Thus journalism demands of its practitioners not only industry and knowledge but also the pursuit of a standard of integrity proportionate to the journalist's singular obligation. To this end the American Society of Newspaper Editors sets forth this Statement of Principles as a standard encouraging the highest ethical and professional performance.
>
> **ARTICLE I—Responsibility.** The primary purpose of gathering and distributing news and opinion is to serve the general welfare by informing the people and enabling them to make judgments on the issues of the time. Newspapermen and women who abuse the power of their professional role for selfish motives or unworthy purposes are faithless to that public trust. The American press was made free not just to inform or just to serve as a forum for debate but also to bring an independent scrutiny to bear on the forces of power in the society, including the conduct of official power at all levels of government.
>
> **ARTICLE II—Freedom of the Press.** Freedom of the press belongs to the people. It must be defended against encroachment or assault from any quarter, public or private. Journalists must be constantly alert to see that the public's business is conducted in public. They must be vigilant against all who would exploit the press for selfish purposes.
>
> **ARTICLE III—Independence.** Journalists must avoid impropriety and the appearance of impropriety as well as any conflict of interest or the

appearance of conflict. They should neither accept anything nor pursue any activity that might compromise or seem to compromise their integrity.

ARTICLE IV—Truth and Accuracy. Good faith with the reader is the foundation of good journalism. Every effort must be made to assure that the news content is accurate, free from bias and in context, and that all sides are presented fairly. Editorials, analytical articles and commentary should be held to the same standards of accuracy with respect to facts as news reports. Significant errors of fact, as well as errors of omission, should be corrected promptly and prominently.

ARTICLE V—Impartiality. To be impartial does not require the press to be unquestioning or to refrain from editorial expression. Sound practice, however, demands a clear distinction for the reader between news reports and opinion. Articles that contain opinion or personal interpretation should be clearly identified.

ARTICLE VI—Fair Play. Journalists should respect the rights of people involved in the news, observe the common standards of decency and stand accountable to the public for the fairness and accuracy of their news reports. Persons publicly accused should be given the earliest opportunity to respond. Pledges of confidentiality to news sources must be honored at all costs, and therefore should not be given lightly. Unless there is clear and pressing need to maintain confidences, sources of information should be identified.

These principles are intended to preserve, protect and strengthen the bond of trust and respect between American journalists and the American people, a bond that is essential to sustain the grant of freedom entrusted to both by the nation's founders.

---

* American Society of Newspaper Editors, Statement of Principles. Reston, VA: American Society of Newspaper Editors, 2002 (last updated). Available at *http://www.asne.org/ index.cfm?ID=888*. Reprinted with permission.

(*continued from page 39*)

made comments that some interpreted as an endorsement of racial segregation. When his comments were made public, thanks in large part to bloggers, Lott was forced to step down as the Senate's Republican leader.

> • **Should bloggers be held to the same standards of ethics as traditional journalists?**

Other factors also curb bias.

Defenders of the media accuse critics of focusing on the wrong target. They maintain that any liberal bias on the part of journalists is more than offset by the conservative biases of media corporations for which they work. Critics cite journalists' Democratic leanings as evidence of their bias, but a survey by *Editor & Publisher* magazine found that, in 2000, publishers favored George W. Bush over Al Gore by a three-to-one majority and publishers and editors together favored Bush by two to one. Some maintain that company owners' and managers' biases are "smuggled into" news stories and made to appear as nonpartisan, even objective, truth. In any event, media companies have no incentive to condone liberal bias. Everette Dennis pointed out that media companies seek the largest possible audience and that they are afraid to offend any substantial portion of the public. As a result, "News organizations would be shooting themselves in the foot by producing a politically-charged, left-leaning product certain to offend more than half their audience. Politically tainted journalism is simply bad business." [28]

It has also been said that "you're only as liberal as the man who owns you." Today, most elite journalists work for companies controlled by six major corporations: AOL Time Warner, Disney, Viacom, General Electric, News Corporation, and Bertelsmann. Many believe that those corporations' conservative values influence what is reported. Robert McChesney, a professor at the University of Illinois, and John Bellamy Foster, a professor at the University of Oregon, argued, "In commercial media, the owners hire and fire and they determine the budgets and the overarching aims of the enterprise. Successful journalists, and certainly those who rise to the top of the profession, tend to internalize the values of those who own and control the enterprise."[29]

There is evidence that corporate values influence reporting. According to a 2000 survey by the Pew Research Center, 41 percent of journalists—including senior editors and executives—said that they were pressured to avoid, or at least tone down, newsworthy stories. Investigative journalists and local reporters were the most likely to report such incidents. Most of the pressure was subtle and came from higher-ups, not from fellow journalists. That same year, an editorial in the *Columbia Journalism Review* warned, "The truth about self-censorship is that it is widespread, as common in newsrooms as deadline pressure, a virus that eats away at the journalistic mission."[30]

Good reporting is unfairly labeled "bias."

The very nature of journalism—acting as a check on wrongdoing by the powerful—invites accusations of bias. As Professor Graber observed, "Pulitzer Prizes and other honors go to journalists who have successfully exposed questionable practices in the interest of social improvement. The most prominent 'villains' targeted for exposure are usually big government and big business."[31] Thus an antiestablishment stance is automatically—and often wrongly—labeled "liberal bias."

Furthermore, journalism is very much an art: Editors have a great deal of leeway in deciding what stories are reported, and journalists have considerable discretion in reporting them. Eric Alterman contended that critics are too eager to call those decisions biased:

The mere fact of paying more attention to a story than an audience would likely choose—as clearly seems to be the case with both campaign finance reform and the death penalty—is hardly evidence of a bias on one side

Walter Cronkite Calls Vietnam a "Stalemate"

In early 1968, while he was the anchor of the *CBS Evening News,* Walter Cronkite traveled to Vietnam to report on the aftermath of the Tet Offensive, an all-out Viet Cong attack on American and South Vietnamese forces. The Viet Cong took control of a number of cities, although they were eventually driven out by American and South Vietnamese forces and suffered heavy casualties.

On February 27, after returning home, Cronkite went on the air to offer his "speculative, personal, and subjective" assessment of the war.[*] In his view, the upcoming battles would result in "a terrible loss in American lives" but the enemy would gain little ground against American forces—a standoff. Cronkite then said:

> Who won and who lost in the great Tet offensive against the cities? I'm not sure. The Vietcong did not win by a knockout, but neither did we. The referees of history may make it a draw.…On the political front, past performance gives no confidence that the Vietnamese government can cope with its problems, now compounded by the attack on the cities. It may not fall, it may hold on, but it probably won't show the dynamic qualities demanded of this young nation. Another standoff.

Cronkite dismissed the optimistic predictions of American and South Vietnamese military officials. At the same time, he said that the Communists had realized that they could not win, even if Vietnam turned into a war of attrition. He continued:

> For it seems now more certain than ever that the bloody experience of Vietnam is to end in a stalemate. This summer's almost certain standoff will either end in real give-and-take negotiations or terrible escalation; and for every means we have to escalate, the enemy can match us, and that applies to invasion of the North, the use of nuclear weapons, or the mere

or the other. It is merely evidence of editorial judgment—something a democracy depends on journalists
to do in spite of, rather than in accord with, market
pressures.[32]

commitment of one hundred, or two hundred, or three hundred thousand
more American troops to the battle. And with each escalation, the world
comes closer to the brink of cosmic disaster.

Rejecting claims that the United States was either winning the war or on the
edge of losing it, he concluded:

To say that we are mired in stalemate seems the only realistic, yet unsatisfactory, conclusion. On the off chance that military and political analysts
are right, in the next few months we must test the enemy's intentions, in
case this is indeed his last big gasp before negotiations. But it is increasingly clear to this reporter that the only rational way out then will be to
negotiate, not as victors, but as an honorable people who lived up to their
pledge to defend democracy, and did the best they could.

Cronkite's remarks caused a sharp drop in public support for the war and were
one factor in President Lyndon Johnson's announcement on March 31 that he
would not seek reelection. Conservatives accused Cronkite of having ignored
evidence that the Tet Offensive was a failure for the Viet Cong and of giving
Americans an unfairly negative picture of the war. Journalists Amy Goodman
and David Goodman disagree. They argued, "It became an article of faith that
'the media lost Vietnam'—as if the American public would otherwise have gladly
accepted the staggering toll of 58,000 Americans killed, 300,000 wounded,
and at least two million Vietnamese killed in a pointless war."[**]

* Ward Just, *Reporting Vietnam: Part One: American Journalism 1959–1969*. New York:
Literary Classics of the United States, 1998, pp. 581–582.

** Amy Goodman and David Goodman, *The Exception to the Rulers: Exposing Oily Politicians,
War Profiteers, and the Media That Love Them.* New York: Hyperion, 2004, p. 170.

Many Americans dismiss tough-minded reporting that they would rather not hear as biased. As former *Washington Post* editor Ben Bradlee explained, such reporting is "not for everyone," and not "for those who feel that all's right with the world, not for those whose cows are sacred, and surely not for those who fear the violent contradictions of our time."[33]

Finally, many Americans do not understand the concept of "objectivity." They wrongly assume that it requires giving equal attention to both sides of a story, even when most of the facts lie on one side. As former PBS journalist Bill Moyers explained, "Objectivity means being true to your own reading of the record and your own analytical processes of reasoning and

Basic Principles of Journalism

Bill Kovach and Tom Rosenstiel, the chairman and vice chairman, respectively, of the Committee of Concerned Journalists, are the authors of *The Elements of Journalism*. This book reduced the principles of journalism, in their most ideal form, to these:

1. Journalism's first obligation is to the truth.
2. Its first loyalty is to citizens.
3. Its essence is a discipline of verification.
4. Its practitioners must maintain an independence from those they cover.
5. It must serve as an independent monitor of power.
6. It must provide a forum for public criticism and compromise.
7. It must strive to make the significant interesting and relevant.
8. It must keep the news comprehensive and proportional.
9. Its practitioners must be allowed to exercise their personal conscience.*

* Robert W. McChesney and John Bellamy Foster, "The 'Left-Wing' Media?," *Monthly Review* 55:2, 1 (June 2003).

conclusion and logic. It's a journalist's job to tell the viewers or the readers what he has come to think about what they see as only data or information."[34]

> • **Do journalists slant their stories to fit their audience's political views?**

Summary

Charges of liberal bias on the part of journalists are exaggerated. Critics unfairly base their accusations on journalists' positions on a handful of social issues and ignore their more conservative views on other questions. They also confuse good journalism—which entails questioning authority—with political bias. Even assuming that journalists are biased, there are ample checks against that bias appearing in the news. Those checks include standards of professional ethics, criticism from peers, and, especially, the conservative biases of the companies they work for. Finally, even when journalists' biases do appear in their reporting, it is debatable whether they have an effect on public opinion.

The Media Have a Liberal Bias

Americans have never held a lower opinion of the media than they do today. As investigative reporter Timothy Maier noted:

> For two decades polls increasingly have indicated public dismay at the spin and fantasies of the press. In fact, a recent Gallup Poll says Americans rate the trustworthiness of journalists at about the level of politicians and as only slightly more credible than used-car salesmen. The poll suggests that only 21 percent of Americans believe journalists have high ethical standards, ranking them below auto mechanics but tied with members of Congress.[35]

Critics maintain that the public has discovered how out of step the media are with the rest of the country and, more important, how blatantly and consistently they slant their reporting to favor a liberal point of view. They add that Americans now tend to view the media as arrogant, disrespectful of their values, and unwilling to change.

The media select stories unfairly.

Brent Bozell, the president of the Media Research Center, insisted that the media are anything but objective: "The media are partisan players. They see their role as journalists as not to inform, but to persuade. They aim to make society better and believe the great society is a society drained of its poisonous vestiges of conservatism."[36] According to Bozell and other critics, one common way of injecting liberal bias into the news is story selection. They contend that stories that support a liberal point of view lead the newscast or appear on page one, whereas those that tend to undermine it receive little, if any, coverage. A famous example, mentioned by Agnew in his speech, was the networks' coverage of the 1968 Democratic National Convention. Broadcasts from the convention showed police attacking demonstrators but did not show earlier incidents in which some demonstrators had provoked the police.

Critics also accuse the media of emphasizing stories such as global warming, gun-related violence, and the outsourcing of jobs to foreign countries in an effort to put conservatives in a bad light. At the same time, stories that tend to discredit the liberal point of view are routinely suppressed. Author William McGowan contends that stories about welfare dependency among immigrants, gay men who practice unsafe sex, and female soldiers sent to war zones despite their lacking the required physical strength, rarely appear in the news. The reason, in his view, is "political correctness" on the part of media outlets.

Another complaint is that many news stories express a liberal point of view through spokespersons. Jeffrey Friedman, the editor of *Critical Review* magazine, contended that "reporters put their views into the mouths of experts so they can appear to be taking adequate account of the world's complexity."[37] Quoting the views of experts creates the impression of objectivity, but many experts are themselves biased, and, because they tend to come from heavily Democratic college faculties, their bias is usually on the liberal side.

> • **Should reporters disclose their own biases? Those of the spokespersons they quote?**

Types of Bias

Brent Baker, of the Media Research Center, an advocacy organization that has monitored and reported on liberal media bias since 1987, is the author of *How to Identify, Expose, and Correct Liberal Media Bias*. In that book, Baker identified a number of forms that liberal media bias might take.

- **Bias by commission.** Passing along errors or false assumptions that support a particular viewpoint. Example: Reporting that the first Bush administration cut funding for social programs when in fact social spending rose dramatically.

- **Bias by omission.** Ignoring facts that tend to disprove one side of the argument or support the other side. Example: Not mentioning former South African President Nelson Mandela's Communist past.

- **Bias by story selection.** Highlighting news stories that coincide with one side's agenda while ignoring stories that coincide with the opposite side's agenda. Example: Highlighting studies that show that the rich got tax breaks during the Reagan administration while not reporting studies that show that the rich paid more taxes during that time.

- **Bias by placement.** Giving prominent placement to stories that support one point of view while "burying" stories that support the opposite one. Example: Placing a story about an abortion-rights rally on page one while placing a story about an equally large pro-life rally in the back pages.

- **Bias by selection of sources.** Quoting more sources that support one viewpoint over another or using phrases such as "experts

Liberal views are injected into reporting.

According to critics, the media openly favor the liberal point of view on numerous issues. They include the following.

- **Abortion**. In 1990, David Shaw, a reporter at the *Los Angeles Times*, studied broadcast networks' and major newspapers' reporting on abortion. He

believe," "observers say," and "most people think" to support a viewpoint. Example: Quoting numerous critics of Pope John Paul II and hardly any of his supporters in a story on his 1993 visit to the United States.

- **Bias by spin**. Emphasizing aspects of a story favorable to one side without noting aspects favorable to the other. Example: Reporting that President Clinton's approval had "bottomed out," implying that it had stopped falling, when in fact it reached an all-time low.

- **Bias by labeling**. Attaching a label to one side but not to the other, using more extreme labeling for one side than the other, or using a phrase such as "expert" or "independent" to identify someone who has taken a position in a controversy. Examples: Calling Concerned Women for America "conservative" but not calling the National Organization for Women "liberal"; calling abortion rights supporters "pro-choice" but calling opponents "anti-abortion"; calling People for the American Way, a liberal organization, "nonpartisan."

- **Bias by policy recommendation or condemnation**. Injecting the reporter's opinion as to whether a policy should be enacted. Example: *Time*'s 1988 "Planet of the Year" story, which included a list of actions that the government "must" take to avoid environmental catastrophe. Some actions, such as raising the tax on gasoline, were on the agenda of liberal environmental groups.

Note: All of these techniques can, of course, be used by people elsewhere on the political spectrum.

found a pronounced pro-choice bias and estimated that 80 to 90 percent of American journalists favored abortion rights. Brent Bozell went further, accusing the media of not only siding with pro-abortion extremists but also of passing their views off as "mainstream." More recently, William McGowan found that news stories about partial-birth abortions created the misleading impression that they are very rare and performed only to save the mother's life.

- **AIDS**. Critics accuse the media of having exaggerated the threat that AIDS posed to those outside the high-risk groups—namely, sexually active gay males and people who use injected drugs. Bernard Goldberg believes that activist reporters working for mainstream outlets tried to portray AIDS as "everybody's disease." He wrote:

> The activists knew, instinctively, that Main Street America did not see [those in high-risk groups] as sympathetic characters. Junkies died every day, from overdoses and who knows what. So what if there was now a virus that was also killing them. The activists knew that Americans would never lose sleep over drug addicts dying from something called HIV.[38]

- **Hate crimes against gays.** Conservative columnist Andrew Sullivan criticized the media for giving extensive coverage to the murder of Matthew Shepard, who was gay, while ignoring the torture-murder of 13-year-old Jesse Dirkhising by two gay men. Sullivan, who is himself gay, alleged that some in the media had an ulterior motive for playing up Shepard's killing: They wanted Congress to extend the federal hate-crimes law to gays and lesbians. William McGowan adds that some journalists crossed the line that separates reporting and advocacy regarding gay issues. He maintains that, at a 1995 gay and lesbian journalists' convention, activists worked together with journalists to develop a strategy for putting the best "spin" on gay marriage.

- **Homelessness.** Bernard Goldberg believes that news stories not only inflated the extent of homelessness but also suggested that Republican cuts in social programs made the problem worse. He contended:

  > For years, the activists played the media as if they were part of the homeless PR machine. And reporters were more than willing to go along and be yanked around by the homeless lobby. A lot of news people, after all, got into journalism in the first place so they could change the world and make it a better place. Rallying support for the homeless was a golden opportunity.[39]

- **Race relations.** In 1996, the media reported on a rash of arson fires at African-American churches in the South. William McGowan accused the media of inventing a crisis: There were no more fires in 1996 than in other years, more white churches than African-American churches were burned, some perpetrators were African American, and a number of whites who set fires were mentally disturbed, not acting out of racial hatred. Commentator John Attarian cited another example: "Compare the attention given to the June 1998 murder of James Byrd, Jr., by two whites in Jasper, Texas, and the December 2000 murder of four whites by two blacks in Wichita, Kansas. The media lavishly covered the first murder and called it a 'hate crime' but virtually ignored the Wichita murders."[40]

The media paint an unfair picture of conservatives.

Critics assert that labeling—implying that one side of the debate is mainstream and the other is extreme—is another common form of liberal bias. The Media Research Center analyzed the words used to describe two major women's political organizations, the conservative Concerned Women for America (CWA) and the liberal National Organization for Women (NOW). Its study of stories in three newspapers and three news magazines in 1987–1988 revealed that NOW was mentioned in 421 stories and described as "liberal" in only 2.4 percent of them. CWA, with three times the membership of NOW, was mentioned in only 61 stories but was described as "conservative" in 41 percent of them.

Labeling also has been applied to individuals. During the mid-1990s, conservative author Allan Levite searched newspaper archives and found that the phrases "conservative attack" and "conservative criticism" occurred more than four times as often as "liberal attack" and "liberal criticism." He also found that the prefix "arch-," an even stronger suggestion of extreme views, was applied to conservatives more than 20 times as often as it was to liberals. Other critics claim that conservative figures such as director Mel Gibson and country singer Toby Keith are more likely to be labeled than are liberal figures such as documentarian Michael Moore and entertainer Barbra Streisand.

> • **Is it necessary to label people "liberal" or "conservative," or should that be left to the audience?**

Critics also accuse the media of treating conservatives more harshly than liberals. They point out, for example, that many of the same journalists who defended Lawrence Walsh's investigation of illegal arms shipments to the Nicaraguan Contras during the Reagan administration criticized Kenneth Starr's investigation of President Clinton's affair with Monica Lewinsky. Others note that the media ran many more stores about George W. Bush's alleged dereliction of National Guard duty than they did about Bill Clinton's efforts to avoid military service altogether.

The media attack respected institutions.

Many Americans accuse the media of being biased against traditional institutions, especially organized religion. They cite news coverage of the film *The Passion of the Christ* as an example. Christian groups accused journalists of emphasizing its graphic violence and alleged anti-Semitic message while ignoring the story it told and the spiritual awakening it sparked. Another example is coverage of the Catholic Church. Media critics cite a one-sided *60 Minutes* story that accused Pope Pius XII of not doing enough to stop the Nazis from exterminating European Jews and stories that suggest that the Church's strict teachings about sexuality were responsible for priests sexually assaulting young boys.

The military, another institution with conservative values, also has been the target of alleged biased reporting. In 1997, the air force took steps to court-martial Kelly Flinn, a female B-52 pilot, for violating military regulations. Because one of the charges against Flinn was adultery, the media portrayed the case as a modern-day version of *The Scarlet Letter*. Defenders of air force policy pointed out that she had committed serious breaches of military discipline—using her superior rank to break up a marriage—and that adultery was in fact a less serious charge than those she could have faced.

Liberal bias extends beyond news reporting. Professor Graber observed, "Politically relevant information is often conveyed through stories that are not concerned explicitly with politics. In fact, because most people are exposed far more to nonpolitical information, make-believe media, such as movies

(continued on page 58)

FROM THE BENCH

The "Pentagon Papers" Case:
New York Times Company v. *United States*

The Pentagon Papers Case began when the *New York Times* obtained stolen copies of a classified study entitled "History of U.S. Decision-Making Process on Viet Nam Policy," better known as the Pentagon Papers. After the first installment appeared in the *Times,* the government filed suit for an injunction, a court order that banned the publication of any more of the papers. Government lawyers argued that President Nixon, as commander-in-chief of the military, had the inherent power to prevent their publication in the interest of national security. The lower courts temporarily halted the *Times* from publishing the papers.

The case quickly went to the Supreme Court which, in *New York Times Co. v. United States,* 403 U.S. 713 (1971), allowed the *Times* to continue to publish the papers. It concluded that the government had not met the heavy burden of proof required for prior restraint—that is, preventing a person from speaking in the first place instead of punishing that person afterward if his or her speech violated the law.

The Court's opinion was *per curiam,* meaning that no justice was identified as its author. Six of the nine justices voted to allow immediate publication of the papers. Each wrote a concurring opinion that explained his reasons. Justice Hugo Black concluded that the First Amendment absolutely forbade the government to enjoin the publication of important news. He explained, "Only a free and unrestrained press can effectively expose deception in government. And paramount among the responsibilities of a free press is the duty to prevent any part of the government from deceiving the people and sending them off to distant lands to die of foreign fevers and foreign shot and shell."

Justice Black also rejected the argument that national security overrode freedom of the press:

> The guarding of military and diplomatic secrets at the expense of informed representative government provides no real security for our Republic. The Framers of the First Amendment, fully aware of both the need to defend a new nation and the abuses of the English and Colonial governments, sought to give this new society strength and security by providing that freedom of speech, press, religion, and assembly should not be abridged.

Justice William O. Douglas pointed out that no act of Congress barred the *Times* from publishing the papers. He added that the constitutional policy against prior restraint was strong enough to outweigh even the president's power to protect national security. Justice William Brennan concluded that, although freedom to report the news was not absolute, prior restraint was inappropriate unless the government proved that publication would cause specific harm, for example, letting the enemy know when a troop ship would sail. In this case, the government had offered no such proof. Justice Potter Stewart conceded that the president had broad power in the areas of national defense and international relations and that exercising them would sometimes require secrecy. Nevertheless, he concluded that releasing the papers would not result in "direct, immediate, and irreparable damage" to the nation. Justice Byron White found that the government had not proven its case for an injunction but warned the *Times* that it could face criminal charges if it published the papers. Finally, Justice Thurgood Marshall pointed out that Congress had specifically rejected legislation that would have authorized an injunction against publishing the papers, leaving criminal charges against the *Times* as the government's only course of action.

Three justices dissented. Chief Justice Warren Burger argued that the lower courts should have been given more time to determine what was in the papers and which, if any, were so vital to national security that they should not be published. He criticized the *Times* for not having told the government that it had stolen property and for failing to work with it in determining which papers were publishable and which were not. Justice John Harlan observed that courts had little power to second-guess the president's judgment that releasing classified material would endanger national security, but they had nevertheless done so in this case. Finally, Justice Harry Blackmun argued that the lower courts should have been given the opportunity to develop a standard for determining when national security overrode the First Amendment. He also warned of the consequences of publishing sensitive material:

> If, with the Court's action today, these newspapers proceed to publish the critical documents and there results therefrom "the death of soldiers, the destruction of alliances, the greatly increased difficulty of negotiation with our enemies, the inability of our diplomats to negotiate," to which list I might add the factors of prolongation of the war and of further delay in the freeing of United States prisoners, then the Nation's people will know where the responsibility for these sad consequences rests.

In 1997, the air force took steps to court-martial Lt. Kelly Flinn, above, for violating military regulations. The charges against Lt. Flinn, who was allowed to resign without a court-martial, included adultery, lying to investigators, and disobeying orders.

(continued from page 55)

and entertainment television, have become major suppliers of political images."[41] The entertainment industry often casts religion in a negative light. The Parents Television Council found that, during the 2003–2004 prime-time television season, a religious institution or member of the clergy was twice as likely to receive a negative mention as a positive one. Critics also believe that the entertainment industry often turns corporations and their executives into villains. One example is Michael Moore's first documentary, *Roger and Me,* which portrayed Roger Smith, the CEO of General Motors Corporation, as a corporate "suit" who coldheartedly eliminated thousands of factory jobs in Moore's hometown of Flint, Michigan.

> • **Does the entertainment industry have a political agenda? Is it right to mix politics and entertainment?**

Finally, broadcasters and filmmakers have been accused of glorifying sexual practices that many Americans find offensive. When television character Murphy Brown decided to have her boyfriend's child, Vice President Dan Quayle and other public figures complained that the show sent young Americans the wrong message about sex. More recently, shows such as *Desperate Housewives* and *Sex and the City* have come under fire for their

Spiro Agnew Accuses the Networks of Bias

On November 3, 1969, President Richard Nixon went on television to defend the administration's decision to continue the Vietnam War. Moments after he finished, commentators on the three television networks offered their analysis. Much of it was critical.

Ten days later, Vice President Spiro Agnew went on the counterattack.* He warned his audience that no medium had a more profound influence over public opinion than television: It could move the national agenda and turn obscure Americans into public figures. Agnew described those in charge of the networks as "a small band of network commentators and self-appointed analysts" who had already made up their minds when they went on the air to criticize the president.

Agnew accused the media elite of being isolated from the rest of America:

> We do know that to a man these commentators and producers live and work in the geographical and intellectual confines of Washington, D.C., or New York City, the latter of which James Reston terms the most unrepresentative community in the entire United States.
>
> Both communities bask in their own provincialism, their own parochialism.
>
> We can deduce that these men read the same newspapers. They draw their political and social views from the same sources. Worse, they talk constantly to one another, thereby providing artificial reinforcement to their shared viewpoints.

He reminded his audience of the networks' coverage of the 1968 Democratic National Convention:

> But as to whether or not the networks have abused the power they enjoy, let us call as our first witness, former Vice President Humphrey [who was nominated at the convention] and the city of Chicago. According to [political historian] Theodore White, television's intercutting of the film from the streets of Chicago with the "current proceedings on the floor of the convention created the most striking and false political picture of 1968— the nomination of a man for the American Presidency by the brutality and violence of merciless police."

In addition, Agnew criticized the networks for paying too much attention to controversy and conflict:

> How does the ongoing exploration for more action, more excitement, more drama serve our national search for internal peace and stability?
>
> Bad news drives out good news. The irrational is more controversial than the rational. Concurrence can no longer compete with dissent....
>
> Now the upshot of all this controversy is that a narrow and distorted picture of America often emerges from the televised news. A single, dramatic piece of the mosaic becomes in the minds of millions the entire picture. The American who relies upon television for his news might conclude that the majority of American students are embittered radicals; that the majority of black Americans feel no regard for their country; that violence and lawlessness are the rule rather than the exception on the American campus.
>
> We know that none of these conclusions is true.

He urged Americans to fight bias by complaining to the networks and local stations and calling on anchors and commentators to disclose their personal views on the issues.

Finally, Agnew closed by saying, "Now, my friends, we'd never trust such power, as I've described, over public opinion in the hands of an elected Government. It's time we questioned it in the hands of a small unelected elite. The great networks have dominated America's airwaves for decades. The people are entitled a full accounting for their stewardship."

* Spiro T. Agnew, "Remarks on Television News Coverage," November 13, 1969, at Des Moines, Iowa. Available at *http://www.americanrhetoric.com/speeches/spiroagnew.htm*.

characters' loose morality, and many Americans object to prime-time shows that feature openly gay characters, such as *Will and Grace.*

Summary

Although the media claim to be objective, liberal bias inevitably finds its way into the news. Biased reporting takes many forms, some of which are not immediately obvious. The forms include selecting stories that support a liberal point of view and ignoring those that do not, portraying conservatives as villains, quoting spokespersons who are biased, and labeling conservatives as extremists. Biased reporting also puts respected institutions—especially organized religion, the military, and corporations—in an unfairly bad light. Despite repeated accusations of liberal bias, the media have refused to admit that it exists, let alone take steps to eliminate it. As a result, Americans have lost confidence in them.

Claims of "Biased Media" Are Exaggerated

In fall 2003, researchers at the University of Maryland found that 48 percent of Americans believed that U.S. troops found evidence of close links between Saddam Hussein and al Qaeda, 22 percent believed that weapons of mass destruction (WMD) had been found in Iraq, and 25 percent believed that world opinion backed the American-led invasion of Iraq. None of these statements was true. The researchers at Maryland also found that 80 percent of those who watched the conservative Fox News Channel held one or more of those mistaken beliefs—compared to 55 percent for viewers of two more mainstream networks, CNN and NBC.

Before and during the invasion of Iraq, the media strongly supported the Bush administration. Some maintain that their pro-war stance not only misinformed the public but also disproved, once and for all, the assertion that the media have a liberal bias.

Evidence of liberal bias is flawed.

Content analyses such as the one performed by Edith Efron and reported in her book, *The News Twisters*, are a common way of showing liberal bias. Many consider these studies unreliable, in part because bias cannot be measured in the same way as, say, a person's height or weight. Eric Alterman observed, "No content study can measure truth. Philosophers cannot even define it. Most, therefore, do not even try. Content studies, therefore, are rarely 'scientific' in the generally understood connotation of the term. Many are merely pseudoscience, ideology masquerading as objectivity." [42] Many such studies also do not meet recognized scientific standards. Professors McChesney and Foster observed, "Honest scholarship attempts to provide a coherent and intellectually consistent explanation of journalism that can withstand critical interrogation. The conservative critique of the liberal news media is an intellectual failure, riddled with contradictions and inaccuracy." [43] Others add that many conservative critics have a background in politics, not in journalism, raising the possibility that they, too, are biased and inject their own biases into their work.

Some experts believe that conservatives' studies are flawed for other reasons, including focusing on a handful of issues to show across-the-board bias, using overly broad definitions of "liberal" and "bias," and "cherry-picking" data—that is, extracting from their findings only the ones that support their beliefs. As a result, studies of bias often produce conflicting results. Geoffrey Nunberg, a linguist at Stanford University, countered the claim that the media attach labels to conservatives but not liberals. His database search of 20 major daily newspapers found that left-of-center lawmakers are *more* likely to be labeled "liberal," and the same was true of left-of-center entertainers. Nunberg also found that reporters were more likely to quote experts from conservative think tanks than experts from liberal ones.

It has also been argued that claims of liberal bias take on a life of their own. Professors McChesney and Foster, who examined press coverage between 1992 and 2002, found that references to "liberal" media bias outnumbered references to "conservative" media bias by more than 17 to 1. When charges of liberal bias are made that often, many people will assume that they are true, whether or not there is a basis for them. In addition, it has been argued that the media contributed to false claims of bias by failing to stand up to their accusers. Everette Dennis argued, "The credibility of the media is not suffering because of a liberal press bias; it's suffering, in large part, because of the continuing charge of bias that has gone unanswered for too long."[44]

A conservative establishment has arisen.

During the 1960s and 1970s, many conservatives believed that the political and academic establishments had joined forces with the antiwar and antibusiness movements. To blunt their influence, they created a counterestablishment that included scholars, commentators, and an elaborate media apparatus to communicate conservative views to the public. Today, conservatives dominate talk radio, publications such as the *New York Post* and *Weekly Standard* strongly influence administration policy, and the Fox News Channel has a large and growing audience.

The conservative media are so well organized that they, too, can influence debate. Some liberal critics, like author David Brock, liken them to an "echo chamber":

> Today, a false or wrong article in the *Washington Times* is read on the air by Rush Limbaugh, reaching 15 to 20 million

people. The author of that piece can go on the O'Reilly Factor, reaching another five to ten million. Matt Drudge, the internet gossip, will post the article, reaching another six million. And that's the kind of racket that liberals don't really have access to.[45]

As Brock observed, some stories spread by the conservative media are inaccurate, if not downright untrue. Nevertheless, by the time they are discredited by the mainstream media, the damage has been done. One example was the Swift Boat Veterans for Truth ads that accused John Kerry of lying about his service in Vietnam. Although the navy's official records contradicted most of the veterans' accusations, the conservative media repeated them so often that some voters believed that they were true.

Some critics also accuse the conservative media of ignoring journalistic standards, especially the ethical obligation to present both sides of a controversy. In fact, Brent Bozell admitted, "Conservative talk-radio hosts, along with conservatives on television like Bob Novak and Sean Hannity, are commentators, not 'reporters' in the 'news' media. Moreover, these conservatives openly, cheerfully acknowledge their biases, something that liberals in the mainstream media refuse to do."[46]

Others accuse leading conservatives of following a double standard: They call themselves "commentators," not reporters, when challenged on the facts; but at the same time, they complain that the mainstream media discriminate by hiring conservatives as commentators but not as editors or reporters.

The media support those in power.

Many believe that the media are biased toward the nation's political establishment, especially on foreign-policy issues. They point out that news coverage consistently favors the administration in power, whether it is Republican or Democratic.

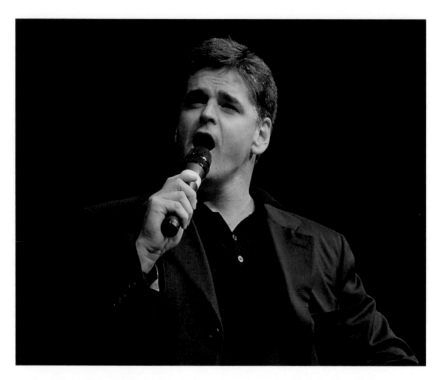

Sean Hannity, above, is a conservative commentator for Fox News Channel. Though the conservative media is often accused of failing to present both sides of a controversy, Hannity is known for openly acknowledging his biases.

For example, during the Cold War between the United States and the Soviet Union, the mainstream media treated pro-American countries more favorably than pro-Soviet countries. As Professor Doris Graber observed, "A comparison of *New York Times* coverage of strife in Cambodia and East Timor and of elections in Nicaragua and El Salvador showed that 'Communist tainted' Cambodia and Nicaragua were judged unfavorably. By contrast, comparable events in East Timor and El Salvador, countries deemed friendly to the United States, were cast in a favorable light."[47] According to critics, proadministration bias became even more pronounced after the September 11, 2001, terrorist attacks. Some of the critics fault journalists for not having asked tougher questions, such as why it was necessary to invade Afghanistan and whether military action in the Middle East could actually increase the risk of future terrorist attacks.

Critics also fault the media for biased coverage of the Iraq war. During the war's first three weeks, the liberal organization Fairness and Accuracy in Reporting (FAIR) found that 64 percent of the sources on the major networks' evening newscasts favored the war and only 10 percent opposed it. FAIR also found that the networks relied heavily on official sources, especially current and former American military officers. The networks were accused of biased reporting about the threat Iraq posed to this country. David Corn, the Washington editor of *The Nation* magazine, believed that the White House press corps failed to do its job of questioning the administration:

> Before Bush sent American troops to invade Iraq, there was a critical debate over the nature of the threat Hussein posed and whether he actually possessed WMDs that endangered the United States. The *Post* and its brethren did not sufficiently cover that debate, and, worse, their editors were overly deferential to Bush—even when they had reason to question and investigate fiercely the claims he used to justify a war. How the *Post* covered this issue mattered greatly at the time.[48]

One of the most criticized reporters was Judith Miller of the *New York Times,* who wrote stories that suggested that Iraqi dictator Saddam Hussein had WMD—the principal reason for going to war. Miller's sources were later found to be unreliable.

- **What should be done to reporters who knowingly use unreliable sources or are caught making up stories or copying them from someplace else?**

(continued on page 70)

The *New York Times* Responds to Critics of Its Iraq Coverage

Some opponents of the Iraq war accused the *New York Times* of careless reporting during the months leading up to it. They were especially critical of reporter Judith Miller, whose stories suggested that Saddam Hussein had weapons of mass destruction (WMD) that could be used against the United States. The Bush administration told the American people that Saddam's possession of WMD made it necessary to use force against his regime.

On May 26, 2004, the *Times* responded to its critics. Although it found an "enormous amount of journalism that we are proud of," the paper admitted to "a number of instances of coverage that was not as rigorous as it should have been." Many of the articles it called "problematic" shared a common feature: "They depended at least in part on information from a circle of Iraqi informants, defectors and exiles bent on 'regime change' in Iraq, people whose credibility has come under increasing public debate in recent weeks."

The most prominent of those individuals was Ahmad Chalabi, the head of the Iraqi National Congress. Chalabi had been named as an occasional source in *Times* articles since at least 1991 and had introduced reporters to other exiles. He was a favorite of hard-liners within the Bush administration and a paid broker of information from Iraqi exiles. The *Times* also blamed administration officials who favored military action against Iraq for "complicating matters" by eagerly confirming the accounts of Chalabi and other exiles. It went on to state, "Administration officials now acknowledge that they sometimes fell for misinformation from these exile sources. So did many news organizations—in particular, this one."

Responding to those who attacked Miller, the *Times* maintained that the problem was "more complicated" than individual reporters. It also blamed editors who "were perhaps too intent on rushing scoops into the paper," failed to consider the exiles' anti-Saddam sentiments, and prominently displayed articles based on "dire claims" while burying follow-up articles that called the original ones into question. The *Times* cited several examples:

- Two articles about defectors who described a secret Iraqi camp where Islamic terrorists were trained and biological weapons produced. Those accounts were never independently verified.

- An article that quoted a defector who claimed he had worked on secret facilities for biological, chemical, and nuclear weapons. After the war, American officials took him to Baghdad to point out the sites where he worked but found no evidence that they were being used for WMD programs.

- A lead article, headlined "U.S. Says Hussein Intensified Quest for A-Bomb Parts," that reported on the aluminum tubes that the Bush administration claimed were proof that Saddam was attempting to make fuel for nuclear weapons. Five days later, the *Times* learned that some individuals in the intelligence community had misgivings about Saddam's intentions but buried a mention of those misgivings deep in a story on page 13.

- During the war, a page one story declared, "Illicit Arms Kept Till Eve of War, an Iraqi Scientist Is Said to Assert." The same informer also claimed that Saddam had sent WMD to Syria. The *Times* characterized both of his claims as "highly controversial."

The editorial concluded, "We consider the story of Iraq's weapons, and of the pattern of misinformation, to be unfinished business. And we fully intend to continue aggressive reporting aimed at setting the record straight."

(continued from page 67)

Critics charge the government with trying to influence how the media report on it. One notable example was the "embedding" of reporters inside frontline military units during the Iraq war. A report commissioned by the British Broadcasting Corporation (BBC) concluded that the Pentagon used the media as part of a campaign aimed at boosting public support for the military. The media also were accused of "sanitizing" the war—in other words, failing to show the destruction and suffering it caused. Journalists Amy Goodman and David Goodman described what was not shown on American television: "In the real war, there were devastated communities, overcrowded and underequipped hospitals, dead and dying victims of U.S. bomb attacks. Anguished families dealt with personal losses. It was gruesome and heart-wrenching. Pain and suffering starred in this war."[49] Another example of influencing the media was the Bush administration's use of taxpayer dollars to promote government programs. In early 2005, it was found that several conservative commentators had been paid to speak in favor of the administration's efforts to reform the public schools and encourage those on welfare to get and stay married.

- **Is news coverage of the Middle East slanted? If so, which side does it favor?**

The media also have been accused of probusiness bias. During the stock market boom of the 1990s, *Time* magazine treated corporate CEOs as celebrities, naming both Intel's Andrew Grove and Amazon.com's Jeffrey Bezos "Person of the Year." Some of the same corporations and CEOs who received favorable coverage were later disgraced. Enron and WorldCom went bankrupt, and officials of both companies were charged with crimes. Critics also accuse the media of overemphasizing the stock-market performance of the corporations they covered. As Professors McChesney and Foster observed, "Today most journalists do not consider the affairs of poor people, immigrants, ethnic minorities, and working people the fodder of journalism, whereas the interests (and happiness) of investors are of supreme importance."[50] Even after the Enron scandal broke, critics argue, the media failed to recognize its full dimensions. They point out that news stories focused on the wrongdoing of top Enron officials and paid too little attention to the company's large donations to candidates for office and its close ties to members of the Bush administration.

Some critics also accuse media outlets of tolerating unethical behavior on the part of journalists who work for them. Eric Alterman observed, "More than simple journalistic gullibility was at work here. A number of high-profile journalists found themselves showered with Enron cash in exchange for extremely little work. To some this might look like a bribe—either to hawk Enron's goods or to look the other way should anything appear amiss."[51]

Some journalists have been accused of "buckraking"—accepting generous fees in exchange for speaking to business groups. Alan Murray, a reporter for the *Wall Street Journal,* observed, "You tell me what is the difference between somebody who works full time for the National Association of Realtors and somebody who takes $40,000 a year in speaking fees from Realtor groups. It's not clear to me there's a big distinction."[52]

The mainstream media have become more conservative.

Conservatives' relentless attacks on the media, which include "blast" e-mails, attacks by watchdog groups and bloggers, and direct complaints to network officials and newspaper ombudsmen (officials who receive and investigate complaints), have paid off. Many believe that the mainstream media have

(continued on page 74)

The Biggest Lies of the 2004 Election

FactCheck.org is a project of the Annenberg Public Policy Center of the University of Pennsylvania. During the 2004 presidential campaign, it monitored the factual accuracy of what was said by major political figures and their campaigns.

A few days before the election, FactCheck.org's staff listed the worst misrepresentations of the general election campaign.* Those made by President Bush's campaign included these:

- **Senator Kerry favored government-run health care.** Ninety-seven percent of Americans with private health insurance would keep it under Kerry's plan.

- **Kerry wanted to raise Americans' taxes.** Kerry said that he would raise taxes only on those making $200,000 or more per year and promised tax cuts for some who make less than that.

- **Kerry voted to slash intelligence spending in the face of terrorism.** Kerry voted for a 4 percent reduction in 1994—a time when some Republicans favored even bigger cuts in order to reduce the federal deficit.

- **Kerry voted for "reckless" defense cuts.** Kerry voted against several controversial big-ticket weapons programs, but he supported every Pentagon budget from 1997 on.

- **Kerry favored raising the gasoline tax by 50 cents a gallon.** Kerry once told local newspapers that he favored such an increase to cut the deficit, but he neither sponsored nor voted for it in the Senate.

- **Kerry was the most liberal member of the Senate.** One publication ranked him eleventh most liberal over his entire career. Other rankings placed him just to the left of the average Democratic senator.

FactCheck.org also faulted independent pro-Bush organizations for making false statements. It criticized the Swift Boat Veterans for Truth for "dubious" ads that attacked Kerry's military record and accused him of betraying veterans, and also criticized the National Rifle Association (NRA) for a "blatantly false" ad that claimed Kerry wanted to make semiautomatic shotguns illegal and voted to ban deer-hunting ammunition.

The worst misrepresentations of President Bush by Senator Kerry's campaign included these:

- **President Bush had a secret plan to cut social security benefits.** Bush said that he would not cut benefits to those who were retired or near retirement age, nor had he proposed any specific plan.

- **Bush gave tax breaks to companies that sent jobs overseas.** For decades, under both Republican and Democratic presidents, the tax code has provided incentives for corporations—some of which outsourced jobs.

- **Bush's economic record was the worst since President Hoover's.** Although the economy had been stronger during President Clinton's second term, it was still "about average" in October 2004.

- **Bush increased the middle class's tax burden.** The Bush tax cuts reduced the tax burden at every income level.

- **Vice President Cheney profited from Halliburton Corporation's contracts in Iraq.** Cheney, who was Halliburton's CEO from 1995 to 2000, severed his financial ties to the corporation before taking office. He made no money from the Iraq contracts.

FactCheck.org also found errors in ads by independent pro-Kerry organizations. It accused the Media Fund of "serial whoppers," including the claim that President Bush allowed Osama bin Laden's relatives to leave the country when most U.S. airspace was closed after the September 11 attacks, and criticized MoveOn.org for a variety of distortions, for example, that Bush had made it legal to own fully automatic assault weapons.

* Annenberg Public Policy Center, "The Whoppers of 2004," FactCheck.org, October 31, 2004. Available at *http://www.factcheck.org/article298.html*.

(continued from page 71)

moved to the right. Newspapers with a liberal reputation, such as the *New York Times,* have added conservative columnists and op-ed contributors. On television, conservatives are regular guests on—and often dominate—panel discussions about politics, and some conservatives, such as the *Wall Street Journal's* editorial board, have been given their own shows on PBS.

> • **Are critics of the media being fair? Do critics exaggerate or generalize too much?**

In recent years, the mainstream media have relied more heavily on official sources, many of whom are government and corporate leaders with conservative leanings. At the same time, in an effort to sidestep controversy, they have also resorted to an "on one hand . . . on the other hand" approach to reporting. Critics maintain that "objective" stories can be bad journalism, especially when the facts are overwhelmingly on one side. That is often true of stories related to science. According to the American Academy for the Advancement of Science:

> The journalistic norm of balance has no corollary in the world of science. On the contrary, scientific theories and interpretations survive or perish depending upon whether they're published in highly competitive journals that practice strict quality control, whether the results upon which they're based can be replicated by other scientists, and ultimately whether they win over scientific peers.[53]

One example is global warming. The scientific consensus, formed after years of study, is that human beings, not natural fluctuations in temperature, are responsible for higher temperatures. Nevertheless, more than half the stories about global warming give roughly equal attention to both sides of the controversy.

Summary

The media are not as liberal as many conservatives allege. Studies that show bias are flawed, and many who perform these studies are themselves biased. Media outlets take a more conservative stance when they report on American foreign policy and business-related stories. Responding to repeated accusations of liberal bias, the media have steadily moved to the right: They have added conservative voices and toned down their reporting on controversial issues. At the same time, a powerful conservative media establishment has arisen. Unlike the traditional media, many conservative outlets reject traditional notions of balance and some exclude liberal views altogether.

Concentrated Media Ownership Harms the Public

T he rollback of federal rules restricting ownership left many media outlets in the hands of a small number of corporations. Who owns the media? According to Amy Goodman and David Goodman:

> Rupert Murdoch's News Corporation (FOX, HarperCollins, *New York Post*, DirecTV, and 34 TV stations), General Electric (NBC, CNBC, MSNBC, Telemundo, Bravo, and 13 TV stations), Time Warner (AOL, CNN, Warner Brothers, *Time*, and its 130 magazines), Disney (ABC, Disney Channel, ESPN, 10 TV and 29 radio stations, and Hyperion [a publishing company]), Viacom (CBS, MTV, Nickelodeon, Paramount Pictures, Simon & Schuster, and 185 U.S. radio stations) and Bertelsmann (Random House and its more than 180 imprints, and Gruner + Jahr and its 80 magazines).[54]

> • **Do Americans know enough about who owns and controls the media? Should foreign corporations be allowed to own American television and radio stations?**

The Project for Excellence in Journalism adds that 22 companies account for 70 percent of daily newspaper circulation and that 10 companies own 30 percent of the nation's television stations, whose signals reach 85 percent of American households. Media reformers believe that the concentration of media ownership has led to lower standards of journalism, a decline in the quality of debate, and even the silencing of unpopular views.

Media corporations have grown too large.

Today's media industry bears little resemblance to the "marketplace of ideas" that the Founding Fathers envisioned. According to Bill Moyers, "The Founders didn't count on the rise of megamedia. They didn't count on huge private corporations that would own not only the means of journalism but also vast swaths of the territory that journalism should be covering."[55]

Reformers note that media companies not only are large, but they also work together on joint ventures. As a result, they have become powerful enough to keep competitors out. In fact, it has become so difficult to enter the media business that Ted Turner, the creator of Turner Network Television (TNT) and Cable News Network (CNN), recently said that he could not have survived had he tried to start his networks today. In addition, reformers point out that owners of existing media can—and do—fight the introduction of new technology. Broadcasters have lobbied against the deployment of low-power FM stations, which citizen groups could use in much the same manner that citizen-publishers used presses in the Founding Fathers' era. Reformers also contend that media companies achieved their dominance not by offering customers the best product but through political clout, lobbying Congress and the FCC for favorable treatment. Ted Turner considers the current environment unhealthy because it shuts the door on independent companies that could provide new ideas.

> • **Should the United States create a government-owned broadcast network like those in Great Britain and Canada?**

Concentration is also contrary to our nation's longtime broadcasting policy. From the early days of radio, lawmakers

FROM THE BENCH

Monopolies and the First Amendment:
Associated Press v. *United States*

In 1945, most of the nation's newspaper publishers were members of a cooperative called the Associated Press (AP), which collected, assembled, and distributed the news. The AP's bylaws barred its members from selling news to nonmembers and made it all but impossible for a paper competing with an AP member to join. The government filed suit against the AP, alleging that its bylaws violated the federal antitrust laws. The case went to the Supreme Court, which, in *Associated Press* v. *United States*, 326 U.S. 1 (1945), ruled that the AP had violated those laws. The vote was 5 to 3, with one justice absent from Court.

Justice Hugo Black wrote the Court's opinion. He concluded that the AP's bylaws were illegal because they placed nonmember papers at a competitive disadvantage and were designed to have that effect. Black rejected the AP's contention that applying the antitrust laws to the AP would violate its First Amendment rights, stating that, although the Constitution guaranteed that the media would be free to publish, it did not give them the right to join forces to keep others from publishing.

Two justices wrote concurring opinions. One of them, Felix Frankfurter, argued that the AP's bylaws were a form of censorship:

> The interest of the public is to have the flow of news not trammeled by the combined self-interest of those who enjoy a unique constitutional position precisely because of the public dependence on a free press. A public interest so essential to the vitality of our democratic government may be defeated by private restraints no less than by public censorship.

recognized that the airwaves belonged to the people. According to the New America Foundation, the electromagnetic spectrum is worth more than three quarters of a trillion dollars. Reformers say that this valuable resource is no longer treated as public property:

> Most of that bandwidth is handed over to corporate interests, used in broadcasting and newsgathering for profit, data trans-

Three justices dissented. Owen Roberts pointed out that two rival news services were comparable to the AP in size and scope of news coverage and that many newspapers used them in addition to or instead of the AP. He also maintained that neither the AP nor any other organization could monopolize news gathering: "The events happening in the world are as open to all men as the air or the sunlight. The only agency required to report them is a human being who will inquire. Surely the supply of reporters is not less difficult to monopolize than the events to be reported." Roberts warned that government supervision of the media's business operations ultimately could erode freedom of the press.

Justice Frank Murphy also argued that the majority's reasoning could endanger freedom of the press. He wrote:

> The tragic history of recent years demonstrates far too well how despotic governments may interfere with the press and other means of communication in their efforts to corrupt public opinion and to destroy individual freedom. Experience teaches us to hesitate before creating a precedent in which might lurk even the slightest justification for such interference by the Government in these matters....
>
> If unsupported assumptions and conjectures as the public interest and competition among newspapers are to warrant a relatively mild decree such as this one, they will also sustain unjust and more drastic measures. The blueprint will then have been drawn for the use of the despot of tomorrow.

mission for profit, and cellular and wireless services, again for profit. . . . Limited, low-power regions are reserved for the public's garage door openers, microwave ovens, and cordless phones—for the people's gadgetry, not their democracy.[56]

Although Congress and the FCC have done away with many regulations, many still believe that broadcasters must act in the public interest, especially given the influence of television. As Doris Graber observed, "There must be assurance that valuable programs are broadcast and harmful ones avoided and that canons of fairness are observed. This is a powerful argument with strong support in much of the world."[57]

Ratings-driven news does not inform Americans.

In 1961, in his famous "vast wasteland" speech, FCC Chairman Newton Minow reminded broadcasters of their industry's Television Code, which provided in part, "Program materials should enlarge the horizons of the viewer, provide him with wholesome entertainment, afford helpful stimulation, and remind him of the responsibilities which the citizen has towards his society."[58] Bernard Goldberg has stated that a network's news division was once considered a public trust:

> In the old days, hour-long CBS News programs, like CBS Reports, tackled the big issues of our times, and producers were not expected to get big ratings. The men who started up the networks in the earliest days of television thought news was special. They made their money on Lucy and Ricky and Jackie Gleason and Jack Benny. For years and years, news wasn't a money-maker and wasn't expected to be.[59]

Today, the ideals of television's early days are all but ignored by broadcasters.

Many believe that today's economics weigh against quality news coverage. The news is now considered a profit center.

Concentration of ownership has resulted in fewer journalists and less money and other resources for covering the news. Financial success hinges on spending as little as possible on programming while at the same time attracting a lucrative audience for sponsors. The result has been a blurring of the line that separates news and entertainment. As Eric Alterman observed, "The net result has been the viral growth of a form of 'news' that owes more to sitcoms and theme parks than to old-fashioned ideas of public and civic life."[60] During much of 2004, the news media—especially the cable networks—intensely covered the trial of Scott Peterson, who was accused of murdering his wife, Laci, and their unborn child. The Peterson trial received far more coverage than more serious legal issues such as the status of military detainees at Guantànamo and whether gay men and lesbians should be allowed to marry.

Some also point to another disturbing trend: hiring commentators who come from the world of politics. Many such commentators are well-known and entertaining, but they have little or no journalistic training.

Reformers accuse media corporations of ignoring the public interest by gutting locally based programming, especially local news. In early 2002, a freight train derailed near Minot, North Dakota, releasing a cloud of toxic anhydrous ammonia over the city. The police tried to call local radio stations, six of which were owned by Clear Channel Communications. According to news reports, it took them more than an hour to reach someone at Clear Channel, whose headquarters are in Texas. By the next day, 300 people had been hospitalized, many of them partially blinded by the ammonia, and pets and livestock had died.

Concentration results in biased reporting.

Most large media corporations are conglomerates—that is, they own non-media-related businesses as well as media outlets. ABC News is owned by the Walt Disney Company, NBC News by the General Electric Company, and CNN by Time Warner, Inc.

Reformers argue that the ownership of nonmedia businesses creates conflicts of interest in the newsroom. Charles Layton, a senior writer at the *American Journalism Review*, observed, "[Conglomerates'] interests are so diverse as to touch on nearly every big issue newspeople cover—tax policy, health care, environmental regulation, insurance regulation, financial services regulation, labor law, equal employment opportunity rules, defense spending, global trade policy and even sports."[61] With such a wide-ranging agenda, a conglomerate is tempted to encourage biased reporting by the journalists who work for it. That is especially true when the top managers are capitalists, not publishers.

> • **Should there be a limit on the number of media outlets a company may own?**

Conglomerates also have an incentive to downplay investigative journalism and instead use their newscasts as "infomercials" for the products they sell—or even government policies that help their bottom line. Amy Goodman and David Goodman explained:

> Why does the corporate media cheerlead for war? One answer lies in the corporations themselves—the ones that own the major news outlets. At the time of the first Persian Gulf War, CBS was owned by Westinghouse and NBC by General Electric. Two of the major nuclear weapons manufacturers owned two of the major networks. Westinghouse and GE made most of the parts for many of the weapons in the Persian Gulf War. It was no surprise, then, that much of the coverage on those networks looked like a military hardware show.[62]

They also have an incentive to look after the interests of their sponsors. In 2001, according to Professors McChesney and Nichols, businesses spent 230 billion dollars on advertising. Much of that money ended up in the hands of media companies.

Media reformers also contend that concentration has hurt independent outlets. Those outlets, which perform an important watchdog function, are either disappearing or being pushed to the margins. Reformers reject the media companies' and the FCC's assurance that vigorous competition still exists. They disagree especially with the assertion that the Internet has "leveled the playing field" and given everyone an opportunity to be heard. As Professor McChesney contended, "While it is true that anyone can start a website, it has proven nearly impossible for anyone to start a commercially viable website unless they are owned by or affiliated with an existing media giant."[63] Some even believe that the Internet gives large media companies an added advantage because they can use their wealth and relationships with other corporations to establish a dominant presence online. Reformers also argue that the Internet provides no guarantee of diverse viewpoints. As Ted Turner remarked, "The top 20 Internet news sites are owned by the same media conglomerates that control the broadcast and cable networks. Sure, a hundred-person choir gives you a choice of voices, but they're all singing the same song."[64]

Concentration endangers democracy.

According to reformers, concentration has resulted in censorship of the news which, in some instances, is as thorough as that practiced by authoritarian regimes. Media corporations have been accused of suppressing stories that expose bad corporate citizenship, such as mistreatment of overseas workers, and cover-ups of corporate wrongdoing, such as the tobacco industry's attempt to hide the health risks of smoking. Without government regulation, little can be done to fight such censorship because the First Amendment applies to actions of the government, not to those of private businesses.

• **Do you trust a free market to provide unbiased news reporting?**

Facing so little competition, large media are able to silence not only what is said on the air but off it as well. In 2003, Cumulus Media banned music by the Dixie Chicks from its radio stations after a member of the group criticized President Bush. Ted Turner observed that the network might not have been so bold if its listeners had more of a choice in country

Challenging Deregulation: *Prometheus Radio Project* v. *Federal Communications Commission*

Beginning in the 1980s, the FCC relaxed the rules that limited the number of television and radio stations a corporation could own. The trend toward deregulation accelerated in 1996, when Congress passed the Telecommunications Act. One provision of the act directed the FCC to review its media ownership limits every two years and determine whether they still served the public interest. The FCC's first review, which began in 1998, resulted in a lawsuit that ended with a federal appeals court ordering the Commission to reexamine its limits on the ownership of television stations.

The FCC widened the reexamination to include several of its other limits on ownership. On June 2, 2003, it adopted a rule that:

- Raised, to 45 percent of the national audience, the limit on the number of television stations a company may own.

- Increased the maximum number of television stations a company may own in a market (the Chicago metropolitan area is an example of a "market").

- Dropped its ban on a company owning broadcast stations and a daily newspaper in the same market.

- Permitted more "cross-ownership." In the largest markets, a company may own television and radio stations, a daily newspaper, and a cable company.

The 2003 rule continued to bar a television station from affiliating with more music stations. Cumulus's action also suggests that media companies have allied themselves with powerful conservatives with whom they agree on many issues, especially deregulation.

than one network, and left intact existing limits on the number of radio stations a company could own in a market.

There was strong opposition to the rule. Two million Americans complained to the FCC that deregulation had gone too far, and two Democrats on the five-member commission agreed with them. Media companies, on the other hand, believed that the rule did not go far enough in easing ownership restrictions.

Media companies and a number of citizen groups filed suit. On June 24, 2004, in *Prometheus Radio Project* v. *Federal Communications Commission*, 373 F.3d 372 (3d Cir. 2004), the U.S. Court of Appeals for the Third Circuit overturned much of the rule. The vote was 2 to 1.

The majority upheld the FCC's lifting of the ban on owning broadcast stations and a daily paper in the same market. It also ruled that at least some ownership limits were constitutional. It found, however, that the evidence did not justify the FCC's specific limits on owning local media.

The FCC had developed a "diversity index" to measure the variety of available news sources in a given market. The appeals court found that index illogical. For example, in the New York City area, it gave a suburban community college's television station the same weight as the ABC-TV station in New York. The court also found that the FCC had given too much weight to the Internet as an alternative source of local news.

FCC Chairman Michael Powell also criticized the majority, arguing that its opinion would prevent his agency from adopting *any* limits on ownership. Ultimately, however, the FCC decided not to appeal.

Many media reformers believe that the public outcry over the FCC's decision to relax ownership limits, and the successful court challenge to them, marked the beginning of a trend toward reregulation. Others disagree. They point out that early in 2004, Congress passed a law that permanently set the television ownership limit at 39 percent of the national audience. That law gave the networks most of what they wanted.

Media metamorphosis

The Federal Communications Commission eased decades-old restrictions on media ownership Monday, permitting companies to buy more television stations and own a newspaper and a broadcast outlet in the same market.

Top television broadcasters

Company	Number of stations	Percentage of household reach
Viacom Inc.	39	38.8%
News Corp.	35	37.8%
General Electric Co.	14	33.6%
Paxson Communications Corp.	65	30.9%
Tribune Co.	26	30.0%
Walt Disney Co.	10	23.6%

Top radio broadcasters

	Number of stations	2001 revenues (in millions)
Clear Channel Communications Inc.	1,238	$3,265.4
Viacom Inc. (Infinity)	183	$2,081.1
Cox Enterprises Inc.	79	$431.4
Entercom Communications Corp.	103	$407.9
Walt Disney Co.	59	$403.9

Newspaper companies

Company	Number of newspapers	Circulation* (in millions)
Gannett Co.	100	7.7
Knight Ridder	31	5.1
Tribune Co.	12	5.1
New York Times Co.	19	3.2
Hearst Corp.	12	2.4

*Largest reported circulation

SOURCES: The companies; The Center for Public Integrity; Audit Bureau of Circulations; BIA Financial Network; Nielsen Media Research; Associated Press   AP

In June 2003, the Federal Communications Commission eased restrictions on media ownership, allowing companies to own more outlets in a given market. Large media corporations have been accused of stifling less popular views.

Finally, some believe that media corporations have become an unelected "fourth branch" of government. They contend that the growth of these businesses is contrary to the Founding Fathers' intentions. In 1945, Supreme Court Justice Hugo Black explained, "The First Amendment . . . rests on the assumption that the widest possible dissemination of information from diverse and antagonistic sources is essential to the welfare of the public . . . Freedom to publish is guaranteed by the Constitution, but freedom to combine to keep others from publishing is not."[65] Reformers also worry that concentration of ownership undermines democracy, which is based on the principle of "one person, one vote." Some believe that a free market in the media has instead established the principle of "one dollar, one vote," which they view as equivalent to letting citizens sell their votes to the highest bidder.

- **Would reregulating the media reduce bias? Is government impartial enough to regulate the media?**

Summary
The Founding Fathers, who believed that freedom of the press would create a "marketplace of ideas," did not envision the rise of powerful media conglomerates. Today, a handful of corporations control most media outlets. Because business owners, not editors, are in charge of these corporations, serious journalism has given way to "infotainment" designed to earn high ratings. Concentration of ownership is destroying local and independent sources of news and has led to programming with a conservative, probusiness bias. It has also resulted in the silencing of opponents and the suppression of controversial stories, both of which could endanger democracy.

The Media Are Healthier Than Ever

When the debate over bias began, a handful of elite media outlets dominated the news. That era ended long ago. As media and culture critic John Powers observed, "People now get their news not only from the broadcast networks or their hometown paper but from cable news, talk radio, webzines, email newsletters, and bloggers, not to mention scores of out-of-town (even French) newspapers they can instantly pull up online."[66] Much of that information is available free of charge to anyone with an Internet account.

Defenders of the free market point out that Americans have never had a wider or more diverse selection of news outlets. They add that the number of outlets would not have grown so quickly had the government continued to enforce obsolete restrictions on the media.

Critics exaggerate the power of media corporations.

Critics have warned against corporate control of the media, but in fact the variety of outlets has steadily expanded. In 1947, for example, a prestigious commission found that concentration of ownership in radio and television had reached dangerous levels. In the years that followed, however, new technology created hundreds of broadcast and cable channels. A similar phenomenon occurred with the print media. Fifty years ago, Americans got their news from a relatively small handful of sources: a local newspaper or two, a national paper such as the *Wall Street Journal,* and a news magazine such as *Time* or *Newsweek*. It was a time-consuming and expensive task to get the news from out-of-town publications. Today, people can go online and get stories—including archived ones—from local, national, and even overseas sources.

Supporters of a free market insist that concentration of ownership is not a serious problem. In the case of television, Adam Thierer and Clyde Wayne Crews, Jr., of the Cato Institute pointed out, "Let's consider some of the numbers that aren't usually mentioned in the debate. Of the 1,721 full-power commercial and non-commercial TV stations in the U.S., Viacom owns only 39 stations, or 2.27% of total. Fox owns 35, or 2.03%. NBC owns 29, or 1.69%. And ABC owns only 10, or 0.581%."[67] In radio, the top 20 companies own less than one-quarter of the nation's radio stations. The film industry is also competitive. After Disney Corporation decided not to distribute Michael Moore's *Fahrenheit 9/11,* Moore found a new distributor, Lion's Gate Films. *Fahrenheit 9/11* went on to gross more than 200 million dollars worldwide, the highest amount ever for a documentary.

• **Does free-market competition act as a check on bias?**

Furthermore, there is vigorous competition among media. A century ago, newspaper barons had more power than the

(continued on page 92)

FROM THE BENCH

The Fairness Doctrine: *Red Lion Broadcasting Co.* v. *Federal Communications Commission*

To address the problem of spectrum scarcity—more would-be broadcasters than radio frequencies—Congress passed a law in 1927 that created the ancestor of the FCC and directed it to adopt rules to ensure that broadcasters acted in the public interest.

Two years later, the FCC ordered broadcasters to provide for "the free and fair competition of opposing views." That policy, which became known as the Fairness Doctrine, generally required broadcasters to air the views of both sides of controversial issues. (The FCC also required a station to offer "a reasonable opportunity to respond" when it endorsed a political candidate for office or personally attacked an individual in the course of covering a controversial issue.)

A dispute over a 1964 broadcast by conservative preacher Billy James Hargis escalated into a challenge to the Fairness Doctrine's constitutionality. Hargis attacked liberal author Fred Cook, who had written a biography critical of Republican presidential candidate Barry Goldwater. Cook demanded free reply time from the station that aired Hargis's broadcast, and the FCC ruled in his favor.

The station's owner, the Red Lion Broadcasting Company, appealed. Red Lion argued that requiring it to air views it disagreed with violated its right to free speech. The appeal eventually reached the Supreme Court, which, in *Red Lion Broadcasting Co.* v. *Federal Communications Commission,* 395 U.S. 367 (1969), unanimously ruled that the Fairness Doctrine was constitutional.

Justice Byron White wrote the majority opinion. He first concluded that the Fairness Doctrine was within the scope of the power Congress had given the FCC. He pointed out that Congress not only failed to stop the FCC from enforcing the doctrine but also in 1959 passed a law that in effect endorsed the FCC's interpretation of the laws that governed broadcasters.

Justice White next concluded that the Fairness Doctrine did not violate Red Lion's right to free speech. As the result of spectrum scarcity, only a few would-be broadcasters could be licensed, leaving the rest barred from the airwaves. Under those circumstances, the First Amendment did not prevent the government from "requiring a licensee to share his frequency with others and to conduct himself as a proxy or fiduciary with obligations to present those views and voices which are representative of his community and which would otherwise, by necessity, be barred from the airwaves." Justice White added that an informed public was also a goal of the First Amendment and that the rights of the audience were superior to those of broadcasters. Without the Fairness Doctrine, he warned, broadcasters could sell airtime to the highest bidder, communicate their own views to the exclusion of all others, and air only the opinions of those who agreed with them. He added that the First Amendment did not protect "unlimited private censorship operating in a medium not open to all."

Justice White also found no evidence that the Fairness Doctrine encouraged broadcasters to self-censor, although he promised that the Court would revisit the issue if it were found that the doctrine reduced, rather than enhanced, the amount and quality of news coverage. He also found that this case raised no question of "the Commission's refusal to permit the broadcaster to carry a particular program or to publish his own views; of a discriminatory refusal to require the licensee to broadcast certain views which have been denied access to the airwaves; of government censorship of a particular program ... or of the official government view dominating public broadcasting," all of which would have raised more serious First Amendment issues.

Finally, Justice White found that spectrum scarcity was still a concern. He wrote, "Nothing in this record, or in our own researches, convinces us that the resource is no longer one for which there are more immediate and potential uses than can be accommodated, and for which wise planning is essential."

Two decades later, the tide had turned against regulation. In *Telecommunications Research Action Center* v. *Federal Communications Commission,* 801 F.2d 501 (D.C. Cir. 1986), a federal appeals court ruled that the FCC—whose members were now opposed to the Fairness Doctrine—was free to repeal it. In August 1987, it did so, finding that spectrum scarcity no longer existed and that the doctrine infringed freedom of speech and was not in the public interest. Congress promptly passed a bill that would have reimposed the doctrine, but President Reagan vetoed it. Since then, attempts to revive the doctrine have failed.

(continued from page 89)

CEOs of today's media companies. Some, like William Randolph Hearst, could move public opinion with what they printed in their papers. (The title character of the movie *Citizen Kane*, who was based on Hearst, told his wife that people would "think what I tell them to think!") Today, Hearst's newspapers would face competition from broadcast and television networks as well as the Internet—none of which existed when he was at the height of his power.

Finally, it has been argued that reducing the size of media companies will not improve news coverage. Large companies tend to have the resources to produce quality journalism, whereas independent outlets often do not. For example, CNN can afford to air money-losing documentaries, hire good reporters and staff, and cover stories from around the world.

The media have never been more diverse.

Professor Doris Graber contended that "any citizen willing to make the effort to get essential current information about a broad array of major issues of the day can find it in U.S. media, though not necessarily in those most readily available to the average person."[68] In television, entrepreneurs have provided the public with content not offered by traditional networks. Ted Turner launched his 24-hour news and headline channels to compete with the networks; later, Rupert Murdoch created the Fox News Channel for those who found the networks too liberal. As a result, most Americans can watch a newscast compatible with their political beliefs. As the *Los Angeles Times*'s Tim Rutten observed before the 2004 election:

> For all intents and purposes, we now have a Republican TV news network—Fox News—and a Democratic one, CNN. According to that Pew survey, 70 percent of voters who say

they get most of their election news from Fox plan to vote for President Bush, while just 21 percent intend to support Senator John Kerry. Among voters who rely on CNN for their news, 67 percent support Senator Kerry and 26 percent say they'll back Mr. Bush.[69]

- **Are CNN, MSNBC, and Fox News Channel biased? Are they more or less biased than traditional networks?**

Internet users can access news from organizations that represent all editorial points of view, including those seldom heard in mainstream American media. For example, anyone with Internet service can access the English-language Website of the Arabic network Al Jazeera, which often expresses strongly anti-American opinions. The Internet has also given rise to a generation of "citizen journalists." With a modest investment, anyone can start a Website. Many believe that online discussions, where strong opinions and personal attacks are common, resemble the political debate of the Founding Fathers' era. They also point out that blogs provide both an alternative source of news and an important check on the mainstream media. John Powers observed, "The best sites cast a hard, steady light on stories the official media have ignored or mishandled; for example, Trent Lott's fall from power was directly due to bloggers such as Josh Marshall and Andrew Sullivan."[70] Furthermore, the interactive nature of blogging makes it possible for readers to point out bloggers' factual errors or continue the discussion that the blogger started.

Finally, it has never been easier to obtain "unfiltered"—and thus unbiased—news online. During the 2004 presidential campaign, a viewer could tune in to C-SPAN and watch the party conventions and presidential debates without commentary. He or she also could visit the parties' Websites and read their platforms and obtain the names of campaign contributors through federal and state election officials' Websites. These Websites also provide a "paper trail" that makes it more difficult for a candidate or journalist to misrepresent facts and get away with it.

The media give Americans what they want.

Conservatives believe that a free market has done what public opinion could not—namely, hold the mainstream media accountable for biased reporting. Brent Bozell observed, "With the rise of alternative media outlets, from talk radio to the Internet to cable television to conservative newspaper columnists, the liberal media can no longer spin any issue as they choose. They no longer dominate, unchallenged and unchallengeable."[71]

A free market also forces the media to compete for an audience:

> Fox is successful because viewers want their news skewed to the right. [Bill] O'Reilly once said, "Conservative people tend to see the world in black and white terms, good and evil. Liberals see grays. In any talk format, you have to pound home a strong point of view. If you're not providing controversy and excitement, people won't listen or watch."[72]

The market rewards outlets that give audiences what they want and punishes those that do not—but it does not make value judgments. Nearly a century ago, sociologist Edward Ross remarked, "Most of the criticism launched at our daily newspapers hits the wrong party. Granted they sensationalize vice and crime, 'play up' trivialities, exploit the private affairs of prominent people, embroider facts, and offend taste with screech, blare, and color. But all this may be the only means of meeting the demand, of 'giving the public what it wants.' "[73]

For better or worse, the same is true today. For that reason, some believe that market forces, not bias, are the real reason for the media's liberal views about race, lifestyle, and sexuality. As John Powers explained, "Because they're in the business of reaching the widest possible markets, media owners and advertisers want publications or programs to be *inclusionary*. Bigotry, or even the appearance of it, is bad for business."[74] In a free market, the public's tastes often trump political ideology. For example, News Corporation owns the Fox News Channel, which has a conservative perspective. The company also owns the Fox Broadcasting Company, which has aired a number of television programs that conservatives find offensive.

Finally, if the audience is large enough, corporate-owned media do air programs at odds with their owners' and sponsors' views. CBS's news magazine *60 Minutes* is a notable example:

> For more than 30 years, local television stations around the country have eagerly broadcast the CBS show "60 Minutes," even though that program takes a relentlessly critical view of corporate and business behavior. Why? Because the program has traditionally had very good ratings and thus increases the prices that stations can charge their advertisers. From the perspective of a station owner, ideological purity is an unaffordable luxury.[75]

Another example: In early 2005, Clear Channel Communications, a broadcasting company known for its conservative leanings, replaced existing programming on 22 of its stations with Air America, a liberal talk network. It did so because Air America could achieve higher ratings.

- **Do journalists have an antibusiness bias? A bias against those in authority?**

A free market, not regulation, is the best approach.

The Founding Fathers believed that, in a marketplace of ideas, the soundest views eventually would win out. In such a

THE LETTER OF THE LAW

Deregulation and Media Concentration

Congress directed the FCC to adopt rules to ensure that broadcasters served the public interest, convenience, and necessity. The FCC responded by enacting strict rules to limit the number of stations a corporation could own. As of 1975, a media company was limited to owning the following:

- One broadcast station in a media market

- Seven AM radio stations, seven FM radio stations, and seven television stations nationwide

- A TV station or a radio station, but not both, in the same market

- A broadcast station or a daily newspaper, but not both, in the same market

Deregulation, which began in the 1980s, led to a gradual loosening of ownership limits:

- 1985. The FCC raises the national ownership limit to 12 AM stations, 12 FM stations, and 12 TV stations. A company's TV stations may not reach more than 25 percent of the national audience.

- 1989. The FCC allows a company to ask for a waiver that will permit it to own both a TV station and a radio station in the same market.

- 1992. The FCC raises the national ownership limit to 30 AM and 30 FM stations. It also raises local limits: In the largest markets, a company may own 3 AM stations and 3 FM stations.

- 1996. Congress passes the Telecommunications Act, which raises the TV marketplace, biased speakers would call attention to their opponents' factual errors and faulty reasoning. As *New York Times* film critic A.O. Scott observed, "In the American media, like it or not, the job of exposing bias is often taken up by people and

ownership limit to 35 percent of the national audience. It eliminates the national limit on radio station ownership and allows a company to own up to eight stations in the largest markets. It also directs the FCC to reexamine its ownership limits every two years.

- 1999. The FCC allows a company to own more than one television station in the largest markets.

- 2002. In *Fox Television Stations, Inc.* v. *Federal Communications Commission*, 293 F.3d 537 (D.C. Cir. 2002), a federal appeals court throws out the FCC's rule that banned a company from owning both a broadcast station and a cable company in the same market.

- 2003. The FCC raises the TV ownership limit to 45 percent of the national audience. It scraps existing limits on the number of broadcast stations a company may own in a market and replaces them with looser and more flexible limits. It also drops its ban on a company owning broadcast stations and a daily paper in the same market.

- 2004 (January). Congress amends the Telecommunications Act, permanently setting the TV ownership limit at 39 percent of the national audience.

- 2004 (June). In *Prometheus Radio Project* v. *Federal Communications Commission*, 373 F.3d 372 (3d Cir. 2004), a federal appeals court rules that some ownership limits are constitutional. It finds, however, that the FCC's evidence did not justify its 2003 limits and orders the FCC to reexamine them.

organizations with a definite point of view."[76] Conversely, a lack of competition invites slanted reporting. Conservative columnist Kay Daly argued that bias is a particular problem in cities with only one daily newspaper because there is no competitor to keep the paper's bias in check. Supporters also believe that a free-market approach is not only flexible but also prevents the media from stagnating:

> Media is a business, with upstream and downstream threats and pressures—disgruntled customers, programmers of content, authors, artists, advertisers, and hostile takeovers. Celebrities bolt. Sports leagues move to new networks. If reporters feel undue influence, they rebel and leave. They can even separate and form a separate newspaper, or join a competitor.[77]

Finally, defenders of the free market maintain that, as flawed as it is, the alternatives are worse. They warn that regulation leads to censorship: "Despite claims about the death of diversity, localism, democracy, and political participation through control in the hands of a few, proponents of mandatory ownership rules in fact advocate their own versions of media control and, ultimately, control of content and information."[78] They contend that, when the Fairness Doctrine was in force, television and radio stations were discouraged from airing political opinions. The rule required broadcasters to provide for "the free and fair competition of opposing views." Given the vagueness of the phrase "free and fair," however, and the penalty for violating the rule—possible loss of one's license—broadcasters shied away from controversial issues. As a result, Americans were deprived of worthwhile debate.

- **Should broadcasters be required to give free airtime to opposing points of view?**

─────●──────────●──────────●─────

Summary

Fears about concentrated ownership of the media are exaggerated. Despite the presence of large media corporations, competition remains strong. In fact, Americans have never enjoyed a wider choice of news providers. New media such as the Internet provide a broad range of views and reduce the influence of traditional broadcasters and publications. A free market ensures that the public gets the news it wants and provides an economic incentive not to engage in biased reporting. A free market is not perfect, but the alternative—government regulation—is even worse. In the past, regulation of the media led to suppression of unpopular views and less-than-vigorous debate on the issues.

Reforming the Media

S ome believe that 2003 marked a turning point in media policy making. A grassroots coalition, whose members ranged from the conservative NRA to the liberal MoveOn.org, protested an FCC proposal that would relax restrictions on media ownership. Ben Scott, a former congressional aide, believes that that was only the beginning:

> Politics cannot stop this issue from recurring in the next session of Congress or undo the exposure of the FCC's practice of conducting important media business behind closed doors and outside the public debate. Nor can politics prevent the energy and public attention spawned in the media ownership campaign from spilling over into other media issues, such as low-power radio, Internet governance, public

service obligations for digital broadcasting, children's programming, free political airtime, and a host of other topics
from spectrum allocation to copyright reform.[79]

In the years to come, media-reform efforts will attract both
conservative and liberal activists.

> • **Has deregulation gone too far or should regulations be scaled
> back even more?**

Is liberal bias still a problem?

Conservatives argue that little has changed since Spiro Agnew
and Edith Efron accused the media of liberal bias. Brent Bozell
recently said of the media, "They simply refuse to acknowledge
that any bias exists. No matter how many times the obvious
is proven, and no matter how many ways evidence is docu-
mented, liberal elites offer denials and prevarications."[80]
William McGowan maintains that the problem of liberal bias
has grown worse. He blamed "diversity" campaigns aimed
at adding minority and female journalists: "At some news
organizations, especially those most committed to diversity,
having liberal values has practically become a condition of
employment. People with more traditional or conservative
views have a hard time getting through the door, and if they do
get through, they are wary of revealing their views."[81]

> • **Is private censorship a serious problem? What can be done
> about it?**

Others maintain that, even if liberal bias existed in the
1960s, it has long since been eliminated; if anything, the media
have moved to the right since then. Professors McChesney and
Foster cite a number of reasons, including persistent accusations
of liberal bias, the rise of the Republican Party's right wing, the
Democrats' move toward the center, media owners' increasing

control over journalists, and conservatives' ability to move comfortably within the corporate media.

Should the government reimpose ownership limits?

Until the 1980s, policymakers believed that a free market in the media was contrary to the public interest. In *National Broadcasting Co. v. United States*, 319 U.S. 190 (1943), the Supreme Court upheld an FCC decision that ordered NBC to sell one of its networks. According to Newton Minow, that decision "has stood ever since as a pillar of the principle that

Proposals for Media Reform

Professor Robert McChesney of the University of Illinois and John Nichols, associate editor at *The Capital Times* (Madison, Wisconsin), offered the following proposals for reforming the media. They consider these proposals "essential—though certainly not exclusive—starting points for mobilizing a media-reform agenda"*:

- Establish a full tier of low-power, noncommercial community radio and television stations across the nation.

- Limit a company to owning one or two broadcast stations and break up newspaper chains' monopolies over entire regions.

- Conduct a study and hold hearings to arrive at fair rules governing ownership of all media.

- Revitalize public broadcasting to the point where it is less reliant on private sponsors and less subject to political pressures and is able to serve less wealthy segments of the public.

- Allow taxpayers to take a $200 tax credit for donations made to nonprofit media. These donations would allow low-power radio and television stations, community broadcasters, and independent the public owns the airwaves, as the legal basis for the FCC's regulation of broadcasters, and as the basis for later Supreme Court decisions on the First Amendment rights of broadcasters."[82] But many argue that the government's "hands-off" approach has not served the public. They maintain that some amount of reregulation is needed to ensure a free press, just as laws against unfair trade practices are needed to ensure a free market. In addition, they believe that regulation would force media companies to refocus on the communities they serve and make it easier for independent outlets to enter the market.

publications such as labor union newspapers to provide serious news coverage and cultural programming.

- Lower postage rates for nonprofit and noncommercial publications.

- To lessen the influence of money on elections, either ban political advertising from the airwaves or require broadcasters to provide free airtime for all candidates on the ballot.

- Ban commercials from local television news and require stations to set aside an hour each day of commercial-free time for news programming, with a budget based on a percentage of the station's revenues.

- Reduce or eliminate television advertising aimed at children younger than 12.

- Amend copyright laws to carry out their intended goals—namely, protecting the ability of creative producers to earn a living and preserving a healthy public domain.

* Robert W. McChesney and John Nichols, "Our Media, Not Theirs: Building the U.S. Media Reform Movement," *In These Times,* April 14, 2004.

Supporters of a free market argue that limits on ownership violate the First Amendment. In *Associated Press* v. *United States,* 326 U.S. 1 (1945), Justice Owen Roberts called the majority's decision to halt a news-gathering organization's anticompetitive practices a potential "first step in the shackling of the press, which will subvert the constitutional freedom to print or to withhold, to print as and how one's reason or one's interest dictates." The end result, Roberts warned, would be that "the state will be supreme and freedom of the state will have superseded freedom of the individual to print."[83] Free-marketers also contend that one proposed reform—breaking up media companies—would do more harm than good. The resulting companies, they warn, would lack the resources to provide high-quality news coverage. They point to what happened after the *National Broadcasting* decision: NBC sold its Blue network to ABC, then a struggling business with a reputation for mediocre programming.

Should the Fairness Doctrine be restored?

For many years, the FCC enforced the Fairness Doctrine, which required broadcasters to cover controversial issues and to air both sides' views. In *Red Lion Broadcasting Co.* v. *Federal Communications Commission,* 395 U.S. 367 (1969), the Supreme Court found the doctrine constitutional, stating, "It is the right of the viewers and listeners, not the right of the broadcasters, which is paramount."[84] In 1987, the FCC repealed the doctrine, concluding that it violated broadcasters' First Amendment rights and no longer served the public interest.

Many, however, consider the FCC's decision a mistake, arguing that it put the rights of broadcasters above those of the public. Some add that it led to conservative domination of the airwaves, especially on the radio. In the *Red Lion* decision, the Supreme Court warned what would happen without fairness requirements:

A licensee could ban all campaign appearances by candidates themselves from the air and proceed to deliver over his
station entirely to the supporters of one slate of candidates,
to the exclusion of all others. In this way the broadcaster
could have a far greater impact on the favored candidacy
than he could by simply allowing a spot appearance by the
candidate himself.[85]

On the other hand, supporters of a free market contend that
the Fairness Doctrine was misused by political parties and
activist groups who filed complaints to harass opponents. In fact,
the *Red Lion* case grew out of a Democratic Party campaign to
discourage conservative broadcasters from attacking President
Kennedy's policies. Free-marketers also contend that the Fairness
Doctrine is obsolete because now there are hundreds of cable and
online news providers that represent nearly every point of view.

• **Should broadcasters provide free airtime to political
candidates? Should the government pay for it?**

Should the government support alternative media?

More than two centuries ago, James Madison urged the government to subsidize the cost of mailing pamphlets and newspapers
so that ideas could be more widely disseminated. Some believe
that today's federal government should lend similar support.
Professors McChesney and Nichols proposed letting taxpayers
take an income tax credit for donations to nonprofit media. A
credit would allow even those who do not itemize their deduc-
tions to earn a tax break by contributing. Those donations, they
suggested, would allow low-power broadcast stations and independent newspapers to provide serious news coverage.

In 1912, sociologist Edward Ross proposed that the million-
aires of his day endow independent newspapers. He believed

that the presence of even a few such papers would force the major dailies to report the news more honestly. Today, some media outlets operate outside the traditional for-profit framework. These include the *St. Petersburg Times*, owned by the nonprofit Poynter Institute; *Ms.* magazine, owned by the Feminist Majority Foundation; and Pacifica Radio, a group of listener-supported stations. Supporters of independent media contend that journalists who work for them face less pressure to suppress stories that would embarrass the powerful or to forgo good reporting in favor of modern-day "yellow journalism."

Will nongovernmental measures work?

Sometimes, government action would either violate the Constitution or do more harm than good. In those instances, it is up to citizens to take action. Vice President Agnew said about bias, "This is one case where the people must defend themselves, where the citizen, not the Government, must be the reformer; where the consumer can be the most effective crusader."[86] Both conservative and liberal activists encourage citizens to complain to media executives about coverage that they consider biased, boycott offending media, and even confront company officials at shareholder meetings.

Some contend that the media are not doing enough to regulate themselves. Newton Minow has called on broadcasters to return to the ideals of the Television Code, which stressed responsibility toward the community, the special needs of young viewers, and the advancement of education and culture. Others dismiss the Television Code as largely symbolic and accuse the broadcasting industry of routinely emphasizing the bottom line at the expense of high standards.

Others believe that more should be done to educate media consumers, especially young people. In 1990, the American Academy of Pediatrics urged more emphasis on "critical television-viewing skills." Today, the United States is the only

Major Trends in the Media, 2004

In 2004, the Project for Excellence in Journalism identified eight major trends in the media*:

1. A growing number of news outlets are chasing a static or even shrinking audience. The only areas to show growth are online, ethnic, and alternative media.

2. Much of the new investment in journalism is in disseminating, rather than collecting, the news. The result has been cutbacks in the newsroom, which could hurt the quality of reporting.

3. Increasingly, audiences are getting the raw elements of the news as the end product, especially on cable and online.

4. Journalistic standards vary even within a single news organization. What airs on an MSNBC talk show might not meet the standards of *NBC Nightly News*.

5. Without investment in building new audiences, the long-term outlook for traditional news outlets seems problematic. If these outlets try to protect profit margins by cutting costs, their audience will shrink even faster.

6. Media convergence seems more inevitable. The trend is for the Internet to converge with older media, not to replace it. The result: Institutions in different media, such as the CBS News and the *Washington Post,* will be competing online.

7. The biggest question may be economics, not technology. If online sources cannot raise money through subscriptions, can they support news gathering on the scale of newspapers or broadcast networks?

8. Sources who would manipulate the press and the public appear to be gaining leverage over the journalists who cover them. With more competing outlets, it is a "seller's market" for information.

* Project for Excellence in Journalism. *The State of the News Media 2004: An Annual Report on American Journalism.* Washington, D.C.: Project for Excellence in Journalism, 2004. Available at *http://www.stateofthenewsmedia.org/execsum.pdf.*

major English-speaking country that does not offer formal media education in elementary and high school, although a handful of school districts do offer courses that explore topics such as film technique, media myths, and journalistic bias.

> • **Have Americans lost the ability to think for themselves? Has it become too easy for the government to spread propaganda?**

Has the Internet reduced bias?

Blogs are one of the fastest-growing sources of news. According to the Pew Internet and American Life Project, about 11 million Americans visited political blogs for news during the 2004 presidential campaign. Blogs are likely to have a strong influence on politics in the years to come.

Bloggers have broken stories not covered by the mainstream media, most notably the story that the Texas Air National Guard memos that criticized President Bush's military service were not authentic. To an extent, bloggers also have served as a check on biased reporting. Experts warn, however, that many bloggers are even more biased than traditional journalists. In fact, a malicious blogger could, in a matter of hours, ruin an innocent person's reputation with lies and personal attacks—and do so anonymously. Jonathan Klein, a former CBS executive, remarked, "You couldn't have a starker contrast between the multiple layers of checks and balances (of network news organizations) and a guy sitting in his living room in his pajamas writing." [87]

Many believe that bloggers should be held to the same standards as traditional journalists—in particular, reporting objectively and disclosing who pays them. The debate over bloggers' ethics intensified after it was learned that, during the 2004 presidential campaign, Howard Dean's organization paid consulting fees to the owners of two liberal blogs that ran stories favorable to him. Although the blog owners insisted that they

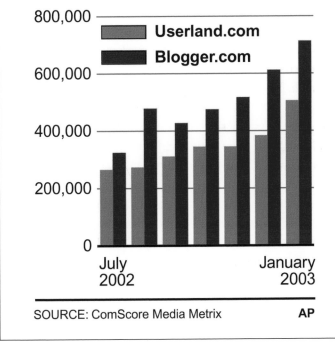

Blah, blah, blog

Some Internet companies are taking notice of the rising popularity of online journals called "blogs" (short for Weblogs). Traffic on two leading blog sites has surged in recent months.

Worldwide visitors

Userland.com
Blogger.com

July 2002

January 2003

SOURCE: ComScore Media Metrix   AP

Blogs, short for Weblogs, are one of the fastest-growing sources of news, thanks to the popularity of the Internet. This Associated Press chart shows how traffic on two leading blog sites grew between July 2002 and January 2003.

did nothing unethical, critics argued that they had a conflict of interest—it appeared that they supported Dean in exchange for money—and therefore should have disclosed the payments. Others warn that bloggers eventually will face the same legal problems as traditional journalists, including being sued for libel or ordered by a judge to reveal sources.

Some bloggers argue that they are not engaged in traditional journalism. "Bloggers should reject the traditional idea of objectivity," said Mickey Kaus, a former *New Republic* and *Newsweek* writer who now blogs on Slate.com. "One of the virtues of blogging is that it's not subject to the professional and bureaucratic restrictions of big media."[88] Others point out that the Internet is self-policing: If a blogger gets his facts wrong or uses faulty reasoning, others will point it out immediately.

Are there too many sources of news?

New media, especially cable television and the Internet, make it possible for Americans of all political persuasions to find the news they prefer. According to the Project for Excellence in Journalism, "Quality news and information are more available than ever before. . . . Some people will likely become better informed than they once could have been as they drill down to original sources."[89] Some also predict that the American news media—which, by international standards, are considered "objective to a fault"—will become more openly biased, like British newspapers, whose political leanings are common knowledge. If that happens, Americans will likely learn to "discount" bias.

Others see a potential downside to having a wide variety of news sources. They fear that people will choose sources—in many cases, biased ones—whose political views mirror their own. Some fear that a fractured news market will result in Americans becoming even more isolated from one another. The *Columbia Journalism Review* recently warned, "We'd rather not live in an America that builds ever-higher and thicker walls between its cultural and intellectual tribes. Such a society won't be stable in the end."[90]

Given both the emotions and the stakes involved, few experts predict that the debate over media bias will end soon. As A.O. Scott observed, "For the foreseeable future, there will be more shouting, finger-pointing and tuning out, as each side accuses the other of bias, distortion and dishonesty."[91]

———————•————————•————————•———————

Summary

Activists of all political persuasions have proposals for reforming the media. Conservatives tend to support free-market solutions that would help create new media outlets to represent all political perspectives. Liberals tend to support government measures, including reregulating media companies and subsidizing independent outlets. Many activists, both conservative and liberal, also support nongovernmental measures such as self-regulation by broadcasters, greater citizen input in media company decisions, and media education for young people. In recent years, the Internet and other new media have given Americans a wide choice of news sources. Many experts consider that a mixed blessing.

Introduction: Fairness, Politics, and American Media

1 Spiro T. Agnew, "Remarks on Television News Coverage," November 13, 1969, at Des Moines, Iowa. Available at *http://www.americanrhetoric.com/ speeches/spiroagnew.htm.*

2 Bernard Goldberg, *Bias: A CBS Insider Exposes How the Media Distort the News.* Washington, D.C.: Regnery Publishing, 2002, p. 3.

3 U.S. Const. Amend. I.

4 *Dennis v. United States,* 391 U.S. 494, 584 (1951) (Douglas, J., dissenting).

5 S.C. Gwynne, "Media Culpa: Should a Few Slipshod, Unethical, Biased Journalists Cause You to Distrust the Whole Lot of Us?" *Texas Monthly* 32:6, 10 (June 2004).

6 Frank Ahrens, "A 'Manchurian' Capstone to Movies' Hate Affair With Corporations," *Washington Post,* August 8, 2004.

7 Robert W. McChesney and John Nichols, *Our Media, Not Theirs: The Democratic Struggle Against Corporate America.* New York: Seven Stories Press, 2002, p. 64.

8 Robert W. McChesney and John Bellamy Foster, "The 'Left-Wing' Media?," *Monthly Review* 55:2, 1 (June 2003).

9 Doris Graber, *Mass Media and American Politics,* fifth edition. Washington, D.C.: Congressional Quarterly Press, 1997, p. 9.

Point: Journalists Are Out of Touch With America

10 Bernard Goldberg, "On Media Bias, Network Stars are Rather Clueless" (Op-Ed), *Wall Street Journal,* May 24, 2001.

11 Eric Alterman, *What Liberal Media? The Truth About Bias and the News.* New York: Basic Books, 2003, p. 12.

12 Agnew, "Remarks," *http://www. americanrhetoric.com/speeches/ spiroagnew.htm.*

13 Brent Baker, *How to Identify, Expose, and Correct Liberal Media Bias,* second edition. Alexandria, VA: Media Research Center, 1996, p. 5.

14 Graber, *Mass Media,* p. 102

15 Goldberg, *Bias,* p. 24.

16 Fred Barnes, "How Many Gays Do You Know?" Op-Ed, *Wall Street Journal,* November 1, 2004.

17 Brent Cunningham, "Re-Thinking Objectivity," In *Our Unfree Press: 100 Years of Radical Media Criticism.* New York: The New Press, p. 296.

18 Baker, *Identify, Expose, and Correct Liberal Media Bias,* p. 207.

19 Alterman, *What Liberal Media,* p. 16.

20 Baker, *Identify, Expose, and Correct Liberal Media Bias,* p. 5.

21 Goldberg, *Bias,* p. 78.

22 Ramesh Ponnuru and John J. Miller, "Helen Thomas: Liberal," National Review Online, May 18, 2000. Available at *http://www.nationalreview.com/ daily/nr051800.html.*

Counterpoint: Journalists' Views Do Not Affect Their Reporting

23 Goldberg, *Bias,* p. 191.

24 Dick Meyer, "You're Biased, I'm Not" Commentary, CBSNews.com, February 9, 2005. Available at *http://www.cbsnews.com/stories/ 2005/02/09/opinion/meyer/main 672653.shtml.*

25 Everette E. Dennis, "Liberal Reporters, Yes; Liberal Slant, No!," *The American Editor* 782, 4 (January–February 1997).

26 American Society of Newspaper Editors, Statement of Principles. Reston, VA: American Society of Newspaper Editors, 2002 (last updated). Available at *http://www.asne.org/print.cfm?printer_ page=%2Findex%2Ecfm%3FID%3D888.*

27 Ben Bagdikian, "The Growing Gap, in *Our Unfree Press: 100 Years of Radical Media Criticism*.New York: The New Press, 2004, p. 278.

28 Dennis, "Liberal Reporters," p. 782, 4

29 McChesney and Foster, "The 'Left-Wing' Media?," 55:2, 1.

30 Alterman, *What Liberal Media?*, p. 24.

31 Graber, *Mass Media*, p. 23.

32 Alterman, *What Liberal Media?*, p. 110.

33 Ibid., p. 267.

34 Evan Smith, "Bill Moyers: The Seventy-Year-Old Journalist—Whose New Collection of Speeches and Essays Arrives in Bookstores this Month—On Why He's Parting Ways with PBS, What it Was like to Work for LBJ, and Whether Objectivity is All It's Cracked Up to Be," *Texas Monthly* 32:6, 92 (June 2004).

Point: The Media Have a Liberal Bias

35 Timothy W. Maier, "The Crumbling of the Fourth Estate," *Insight on the News*, May 11, 2004.

36 Brent Bozell III, "They're Not Referees," MediaResearchCenter.com, October 27, 2004. Available at *http://www.mrc.org/BozellColumns/newscolumn/2004/col20041027.asp.*

37 Jeffrey Friedman, "Honestly Biased," National Review Online, December 22, 2004. Available at *http://www.nationalreview.com/comment/friedman200412220817.asp.*

38 Goldberg, *Bias*, p. 76.

39 Ibid., p. 69.

40 John Attarian, "Who's Guarding the Guards?," *The World & I* 18:6, 212 (June 2003).

41 Graber, *Mass Media*, p. 4.

Counterpoint: Claims of "Biased Media" Are Exaggerated

42 Alterman, *What Liberal Media?*, p. 15.

43 McChesney and Foster "The 'Left-Wing' Media?," 55:2, 1.

44 Dennis, "Liberal Reporters," 782, 4.

45 Transcript, PBS "NOW" Broadcast, December 17, 2004. Available at *http://www.pbs.org/now/transcript/transcript351_full.html#farewell.*

46 L. Brent Bozell III, *Weapons of Mass Distortion The Coming Meltdown of the Liberal Media*. New York: Crown Forum, 2004, p. 57.

47 Graber, *Mass Media*, p. 362.

48 David Corn, "Media Lessons," TomPaine.com, August 18, 2004. Available at *http://www.tompaine.com/articles/media_lessons.php.*

49 Amy Goodman, and David Goodman, *The Exception to the Rulers: Exposing Oily Politicians, War Profiteers, and the Media That Love Them*. New York: Hyperion, 2004, pp. 197–198.

50 McChesney and Foster "The 'Left-Wing' Media?," 55:2, 1.

51 Alterman, *What Liberal Media?*, p. 133.

52 Ibid., p. 33.

53 Chris Mooney, "Blinded by Science: How 'Balanced Coverage' Lets the Scientific Fringe Hijack Reality," *Columbia Journalism Review* 43:4, 26 (November/December 2004).

Point: Concentrated Media Ownership Harms the Public

54 Goodman and Goodman, *Exception to the Rulers*, p. 153.

55 Robert W. McChesney and John Nichols, *Our Media, Not Theirs: The Democratic Struggle Against Corporate America*. New York: Seven Stories Press, 2002, p. 45.

56 Goodman and Goodman, *Exception to the Rulers*, p. 303.

57 Graber, *Mass Media*, p. 398.

58 Newton N. Minow, "Television and the Public Interest," Address to the National Association of Broadcasters, May 9, 1961. Available at *http://www.american-rhetoric.com/speeches/newtonminow.htm.*

59 Goldberg, *Bias*, p. 92.

60 Alterman, *What Liberal Media?*, pp. 24–25.

61 Charles Layton, "Lobbying Juggernaut," *American Journalism Review* 26:5, 26 (October/November 2004).

62 Goodman and Goodman, *Exception to the Rulers*, p. 152.

63 McChesney and Nichols, *Our Media*, p. 76.

64 Ted Turner, "My Beef With Big Media," *Washington Monthly* 36:7–8, 30 (July/August 2004).

65 *Associated Press* v. *United States*, 326 U.S. 1, 20 (1945).

Counterpoint: The Media Are Healthier Than Ever

66 John Powers, *Sore Winners (And the Rest of Us) in George Bush's America*. New York: Doubleday, 2004, p. 194.

67 Adam Thierer and Clyde Wayne Crews, Jr., "What Media Monopolies?" Op-Ed, *Wall Street Journal*, July 29, 2003.

68 Graber, *Mass Media*, p. 382.

69 Tim Rutten, "Campaign's Lasting Effect for Media," *Christian Science Monitor*, November 3, 2004.

70 Powers, *Sore Winners*, p. 196.

71 Bozell, *Weapons of Mass Distortion*, p. 173.

72 Alterman, *What Liberal Media?*, p. 43–44.

73 Edward A. Ross, "The Suppression of Important News." In *Our Unfree Press:*

100 Years of Radical Media Criticism. New York: The New Press, 2004, p. 181.

74 Powers, *Sore Winners*, p. 236.

75 William G. Mayer, "Why Talk Radio is Conservative," *The Public Interest* 156, 86 (Summer 2004).

76 A.O. Scott, "Tallyho! Spin, Flag Waving And Shouting To Catch a Fox," *New York Times*, July 20, 2004.

77 Clyde Wayne Crews, Jr., "A Defense of Media Monopoly," *Communications Lawyer*, 3:21, 13 (Fall 2003).

78 Ibid.

Conclusion: Reforming the Media

79 Ben Scott, "The Politics and Policy of Media Ownership," AM. U. L. REV. 53:3, 650 (2004) 676.

80 Bozell, *Weapons of Mass Distortion*, p. 248.

81 William McGowan, *Coloring the News: How Crusading for Diversity Has Corrupted American Journalism*. San Francisco, CA: Encounter Books, 2001, p. 31.

82 Newton N. Minow and Craig L. LaMay, *Abandoned in the Wasteland: Children, Television, and the First Amendment*. New York: Hill and Wang, 1995, p. 88.

83 *Associated Press* v. *United States*, 326 U.S. 1, 48 (1945).

84 *Red Lion Broadcasting Co.* v. *Federal Communications Commission*, 395 U.S. 367, 390 (1969).

85 Ibid., pp. 382–383.

86 Agnew, "Remarks." Available at *http://www.americanrhetoric.com/speeches/spiroagnew.htm.*

87 Holly Yeager, "Blogs and Bias: How Fragmented and Partisan Media Are Shaping the U.S. Election," *Financial Times*, September 24, 2004.

88 Jessica Mintz, "When Bloggers Make News," *Wall Street Journal*, January 21, 2005.

89 Project for Excellence in Journalism,
    *The State of the News Media 2004: An
    Annual Report on American Journalism.*
    Washington, D.C.: Project for Excellence
    in Journalism, 2004, pp. 4–5. Available
    at *http://www.stateofthenewsmedia.org/
    execsum.pdf.*

90 Editorial, "Red News, Blue News: A
    Search for Meaning in a Fog of Facts,"
    Columbia Journalism Review 43:4, 6
    (November/December 2004).

91 A.O. Scott, "Tallyho!"

Books

Alterman, Eric. *What Liberal Media? The Truth About Bias and the News.* New York: Basic Books, 2003.

Baker, Brent. *How to Identify, Expose, and Correct Liberal Media Bias.* Alexandria, VA: Media Research Center, 1994.

Bozell, L. Brent III. *Weapons of Mass Distortion: The Coming Meltdown of the Liberal Media.* New York: Crown Forum, 2004.

Brock, David. *The Republican Noise Machine: Right-Wing Media and How it Corrupts Democracy.* New York: Random House, 2004.

Efron, Edith. *The News Twisters.* Los Angeles, CA: Nash Publishing, 1971.

Goldberg, Bernard. *Bias: A CBS Insider Exposes How the Media Distort the News.* Washington, D.C.: Regnery Publishing, 2002.

Goodman, Amy, and David Goodman. *The Exception to the Rulers: Exposing Oily Politicians, War Profiteers, and the Media That Love Them.* New York: Hyperion, 2004.

McChesney, Robert W., and Ben Scott, eds. *Our Unfree Press: 100 Years of Radical Media Criticism.* New York: The New Press, 2004.

Miscellaneous

Agnew, Spiro T. "Remarks on Television News Coverage," November 13, 1969, at Des Moines, Iowa. Available at *http://www.americanrhetoric.com/speeches/spiroagnew.htm.*

Cronkite, Walter. "We Are Mired in Stalemate," CBS News broadcast, February 27, 1968. In *Reporting Vietnam: Part One: American Journalism 1959–1969.* New York: Literary Classics of the United States, 1998, pp. 581–582.

Media-Related Organizations
Conservative Organizations
Media Research Center

http://www.mrc.org
Founded in 1987, this foundation conducts studies that show liberal media bias and seeks ways to neutralize the impact of that bias.

TownHall.com

http://www.townhall.com
This is a self-described "one-stop mall of ideas" where people exchange, discuss, and disseminate news from the conservative movement.

Liberal Organizations

Free Press

http://www.freepress.net
This organization favors media reform, including a more competitive industry with a strong nonprofit and noncommercial sector.

Media Matters for America

http://mediamatters.org
This organization is dedicated to monitoring, analyzing, and correcting conservative misinformation in the American media.

Other Organizations

Columbia Journalism Review

http://www.cjr.org
Founded in 1961, this highly regarded publication acts as a watchdog over both traditional and new media.

FactCheck.org

http://www.factcheck.org
This organization acts as a nonpartisan "consumer advocate" for voters. It aims to reduce deception in American politics by monitoring the factual accuracy of what is said.

Federal Communications Commission

http://www.fcc.gov
This federal agency is responsible for regulating the broadcast industry. It enforces limits on corporate ownership of media outlets.

Poynter Institute

http://www.poynter.org
This educational institution is dedicated to educating journalists and promoting excellence and integrity in the profession.

Cases and Statutes

Associated Press v. United States, 326 U.S. 1 (1945).
The Court concluded that the First Amendment did not justify a news-gathering organization's rules that excluded competing newspapers.

National Broadcasting Co. v. United States, 319 U.S. 190 (1943).
The Court upheld an FCC decision that found that a broadcasting company dominated the market and ordered it to sell one of its radio networks.

New York Times Company v. Sullivan, 376 U.S. 254 (1964).
This decision gave the news media broad First Amendment protection by imposing a very high standard for public officials to meet when suing for libel.

New York Times Co. v. United States, 403 U.S. 713 (1971).
The Court refused to stop the publication of classified documents about America's Vietnam policy because doing so would be an unconstitutional prior restraint on speech.

Prometheus Radio Project v. Federal Communications Commission, 373 F.3d 372 (3d Cir. 2004).
The Court concluded that rules that limited ownership of media were constitutional but that the FCC's evidence failed to justify its specific rules that loosened those limits.

Red Lion Broadcasting Co., Inc. v. Federal Communications Commission, 395 U.S. 367 (1969).
This decision upheld the constitutionality of the Fairness Doctrine, which obligated broadcasters to cover controversial issues and air both sides' opinions. The FCC repealed the doctrine in 1987.

Telecommunications Act of 1996, Public Law 104-104.
This far-reaching legislation overhauled the nation's telecommunications laws. It raised limits on how many media outlets a company may own and directed the FCC to conduct regular reviews of its ownership limits.

Terms and Concepts

broadcast license

censorship

concentration of ownership

conflict of interest

content analysis

content regulation

cross-ownership

deregulation

Fairness Doctrine

Federal Communications Commission

First Amendment

independent media

mainstream media

"marketplace of ideas"

mass media

libel

objectivity

"political correctness"

prior restraint

public figure

op-ed page

self-censorship

spectrum scarcity

story selection

talk radio

Telecommunications Act of 1996

Television Code

Weblog

"yellow journalism"

Beginning Legal Research

The goal of POINT/COUNTERPOINT is not only to provide the reader with an introduction to a controversial issue affecting society, but also to encourage the reader to explore the issue more fully. This appendix, then, is meant to serve as a guide to the reader in researching the current state of the law as well as exploring some of the public-policy arguments as to why existing laws should be changed or new laws are needed.

Like many types of research, legal research has become much faster and more accessible with the invention of the Internet. This appendix discusses some of the best starting points, but of course "surfing the Net" will uncover endless additional sources of information—some more reliable than others. Some important sources of law are not yet available on the Internet, but these can generally be found at the larger public and university libraries. Librarians usually are happy to point patrons in the right direction.

The most important source of law in the United States is the Constitution. Originally enacted in 1787, the Constitution outlines the structure of our federal government and sets limits on the types of laws that the federal government and state governments can pass. Through the centuries, a number of amendments have been added to or changed in the Constitution, most notably the first ten amendments, known collectively as the Bill of Rights, which guarantee important civil liberties. Each state also has its own constitution, many of which are similar to the U.S. Constitution. It is important to be familiar with the U.S. Constitution because so many of our laws are affected by its requirements. State constitutions often provide protections of individual rights that are even stronger than those set forth in the U.S. Constitution.

Within the guidelines of the U.S. Constitution, Congress—both the House of Representatives and the Senate—passes bills that are either vetoed or signed into law by the President. After the passage of the law, it becomes part of the United States Code, which is the official compilation of federal laws. The state legislatures use a similar process, in which bills become law when signed by the state's governor. Each state has its own official set of laws, some of which are published by the state and some of which are published by commercial publishers. The U.S. Code and the state codes are an important source of legal research; generally, legislators make efforts to make the language of the law as clear as possible.

However, reading the text of a federal or state law generally provides only part of the picture. In the American system of government, after the legislature passes laws and the executive (U.S. President or state governor) signs them, it is up to the judicial branch of the government, the court system, to interpret the laws and decide whether they violate any provision of the Constitution. At the state level, each state's supreme court has the ultimate authority in determining what a law means and whether or not it violates the state constitution. However, the federal courts—headed by the U.S. Supreme Court—can review state laws and court decisions to determine whether they violate federal laws or the U.S. Constitution. For example, a state court may find that a particular criminal law is valid under the state's constitution, but a federal court may then review the state court's decision and determine that the law is invalid under the U.S. Constitution.

It is important, then, to read court decisions when doing legal research. The Constitution uses language that is intentionally very general—for example, prohibiting "unreasonable searches and seizures" by the police—and court cases often provide more guidance. For example, the U.S. Supreme Court's 2001 decision in *Kyllo* v. *United States* held that scanning the outside of a person's house using a heat sensor to determine whether the person is growing marijuana is unreasonable—*if* it is done without a search warrant secured from a judge. Supreme Court decisions provide the most definitive explanation of the law of the land, and it is therefore important to include these in research. Often, when the Supreme Court has not decided a case on a particular issue, a decision by a federal appeals court or a state supreme court can provide guidance; but just as laws and constitutions can vary from state to state, so can federal courts be split on a particular interpretation of federal law or the U.S. Constitution. For example, federal appeals courts in Louisiana and California may reach opposite conclusions in similar cases.

Lawyers and courts refer to statutes and court decisions through a formal system of citations. Use of these citations reveals which court made the decision (or which legislature passed the statute) and when and enables the reader to locate the statute or court case quickly in a law library. For example, the legendary Supreme Court case *Brown* v. *Board of Education* has the legal citation 347 U.S. 483 (1954). At a law library, this 1954 decision can be found on page 483 of volume 347 of the U.S. Reports, the official collection of the Supreme Court's decisions. Citations can also be helpful in locating court cases on the Internet.

Understanding the current state of the law leads only to a partial understanding of the issues covered by the POINT/COUNTERPOINT series. For a fuller understanding of the issues, it is necessary to look at public-policy arguments that the current state of the law is not adequately addressing the issue. Many groups lobby for new legislation or changes to existing legislation; the National Rifle Association (NRA), for example, lobbies Congress and the state legislatures constantly to make existing gun control laws less restrictive and not to pass additional laws. The NRA and other groups dedicated to various causes might also intervene in pending court cases: a group such as Planned Parenthood might file a brief *amicus curiae* (as "a friend of the court")—called an "amicus brief"—in a lawsuit that could affect abortion rights. Interest groups also use the media to influence public opinion, issuing press releases and frequently appearing in interviews on news programs and talk shows. The books in POINT/COUNTERPOINT list some of the interest groups that are active in the issue at hand, but in each case there are countless other groups working at the local, state, and national levels. It is important to read everything with a critical eye, for sometimes interest groups present information in a way that can be read only to their advantage. The informed reader must always look for bias.

Finding sources of legal information on the Internet is relatively simple thanks to "portal" sites such as FindLaw (*www.findlaw.com*), which provides access to a variety of constitutions, statutes, court opinions, law review articles, news articles, and other resources—including all Supreme Court decisions issued since 1893. Other useful sources of information include the U.S. Government Printing Office (*www.gpo.gov*), which contains a complete copy of the U.S. Code, and the Library of Congress's THOMAS system (*thomas.loc.gov*), which offers access to bills pending before Congress as well as recently passed laws. Of course, the Internet changes every second of every day, so it is best to do some independent searching. Most cases, studies, and opinions that are cited or referred to in public debate can be found online— and *everything* can be found in one library or another.

The Internet can provide a basic understanding of most important legal issues, but not all sources can be found there. To find some documents it is necessary to visit the law library of a university or a public law library; some cities have public law libraries, and many library systems keep legal documents at the main branch. On the following page are some common citation forms.

COMMON CITATION FORMS

Source of Law	Sample Citation	Notes
U.S. Supreme Court	*Employment Division v. Smith*, 485 U.S. 660 (1988)	The U.S. Reports is the official record of Supreme Court decisions. There is also an unofficial Supreme Court ("S. Ct.") reporter.
U.S. Court of Appeals	*United States v. Lambert*, 695 F.2d 536 (11th Cir.1983)	Appellate cases appear in the Federal Reporter, designated by "F." The 11th Circuit has jurisdiction in Alabama, Florida, and Georgia.
U.S. District Court	*Carillon Importers, Ltd. v. Frank Pesce Group, Inc.*, 913 F.Supp. 1559 (S.D.Fla.1996)	Federal trial-level decisions are reported in the Federal Supplement ("F. Supp."). Some states have multiple federal districts; this case originated in the Southern District of Florida.
U.S. Code	Thomas Jefferson Commemoration Commission Act, 36 U.S.C., §149 (2002)	Sometimes the popular names of legislation—names with which the public may be familiar—are included with the U.S. Code citation.
State Supreme Court	*Sterling v. Cupp*, 290 Ore. 611, 614, 625 P.2d 123, 126 (1981)	The Oregon Supreme Court decision is reported in both the state's reporter and the Pacific regional reporter.
State Statute	Pennsylvania Abortion Control Act of 1982, 18 Pa. Cons. Stat. 3203-3220 (1990)	States use many different citation formats for their statutes.

Market. *See* Free market
Marshall, Thurgood,
57
McChesney, Robert
on conservative
critique of media,
63, 64
on corporate owner-
ship of media,
42–43
on journalists' reports
on wealthy,
70–71
proposals for media
reform, 102–103
on success of web-
sites, 83
McGowan, William,
49, 52, 53, 101
Media. *See also* Corpo-
rate ownership of
media
broadcast media's
initial years, 18–19
in colonial America,
13–16, 87
democracy and,
83–87
future issues involv-
ing, 100–101
2004 trends, 107
Media concentration.
See Corporate own-
ership of media
Media critics on staff,
39
Media education for
children, 106–107,
108, 110
Media Fund, 73
Media Matters for
America, 39
The Media Monopoly
(Bagdikian), 39

Media-reform agenda,
102–103, 111
Media Research Center,
39, 54
Memogate Scandal of
CBS, 33–34
Meyer, Dick, 37
Military, alleged biased
reporting on, 55
Miller, Judith, 67–69
Minot, ND, train
derailment, 81
Minow, Newton, 80,
106
Monopolies, 78–79
Moore, Michael, 58
MoveOn.org, 73
Moyers, Bill, 46–47, 77
Ms. (magazine), 106
Muckraker journalists,
17
Murphy, Frank, 79
Murray, Alan, 71

*National Broadcasting
Co. v. United States,*
102–103
National Organization
for Women (NOW),
54
National Rifle Associa-
tion (NRA), 73
National security versus
freedom of the press,
56
NBC, 82, 89, 102–103
Networks, Agnew's
description of, 59
New Class in America,
26–27
New York Times,
68–69, 74
New York Times Co.,
86

*New York Times Co. v.
Sullivan,* 19–21
*New York Times Co. v.
United States,* 56–57
*New York Weekly
Journal* (newspaper),
14
News commentators,
65, 81
News Corporation, 95
The News Twisters
(Efron), 30–31, 63
Nichols, John, 102–103
Nixon, Richard, 32, 59
Nongovernmental
measures, 106–107
Nonprofit media,
105–106
North American Free
Trade Agreement
(NAFTA), 37
Nunberg, Geoffrey,
63–64

Objectivity
critics of, 74, 110
definition of, 46–47,
63
Official sources of
information, 67–70,
74
Omission, bias by, 50
O'Reilly, Bill, 94
O'Reilly Factor, 64–65
Orlando Sentinel, 35
OxyContin news story,
35

Pacifica Radio, 106
Pack-mentality, 26
Parents Television
Council, 58
Partisan journalism,
17

page:
 12: Associated Press, AP
 27: Associated Press, AP/Gregory Bull
 58: Associated Press, AP/Darrel Ellis

 66: Associated Press, AP/Frank Bott
 86: Associated Press Graphics
 109: Associated Press Graphics

Cover: © Chuck Savage/CORBIS

PAUL RUSCHMANN, J.D., is a legal analyst and writer based in Canton, Michigan. He received his undergraduate degree from the University of Notre Dame and his law degree from the University of Michigan. He is a member of the State Bar of Michigan. His areas of specialization include legislation, public safety, traffic and transportation, and trade regulation. He is also the author of *Legalizing Marijuana, Mandatory Military Service, The War on Terror, The FCC and Regulating Indecency,* and *Tort Reform,* other titles in the POINT/COUNTERPOINT series. He can be found on line at www.PaulRuschmann.com.

ALAN MARZILLI, M.A., J.D., of Durham, North Carolina, is an independent consultant working on several ongoing projects for state and federal government agencies and nonprofit organizations. He has spoken about mental health issues in thirty states, the District of Columbia, and Puerto Rico; his work includes training mental health administrators, nonprofit management and staff, and people with mental illness and their family members on a wide variety of topics, including effective advocacy, community-based mental health services, and housing. He has written several handbooks and training curricula that are used nationally. He managed statewide and national mental health advocacy programs and worked for several public interest lobbying organizations in Washington, D.C., while studying law at Georgetown University.